THE ENOCH EXPERIENCE

How To Walk With God

NAIDA M. PARSON, PH.D

WESTBOW
PRESS®
A DIVISION OF THOMAS NELSON
& ZONDERVAN

WestBow Press books may be ordered through booksellers or by contacting:

WestBow Press
A Division of Thomas Nelson & Zondervan
1663 Liberty Drive
Bloomington, IN 47403
www.westbowpress.com
844-714-3454

Because of the dynamic nature of the Internet, any web addresses or links contained in this book may have changed since publication and may no longer be valid. The views expressed in this work are solely those of the author and do not necessarily reflect the views of the publisher, and the publisher hereby disclaims any responsibility for them.

Any people depicted in stock imagery provided by Getty Images are models, and such images are being used for illustrative purposes only.
Certain stock imagery © Getty Images.

Scripture taken from the King James Version of the Bible.

Scripture quotations taken from The Holy Bible, New International Version® NIV® Copyright © 1973 1978 1984 2011 by Biblica, Inc. TM. Used by permission. All rights reserved worldwide.

Scripture taken from The Message. Copyright © 1993, 1994, 1995, 1996, 2000, 2001, 2002. Used by permission of NavPress Publishing Group.

Scriptures and additional materials quoted are from the Good News Bible © 1994 published by the Bible Societies/HarperCollins Publishers Ltd UK, Good News Bible© American Bible Society 1966, 1971, 1976, 1992. Used with permission.

Scripture taken from the Amplified Bible, Copyright © 1954, 1958, 1962, 1964, 1965, 1987 by The Lockman Foundation. Used with permission.

"Scripture quotations are from the ESV® Bible (The Holy Bible, English Standard Version®), copyright © 2001 by Crossway, a publishing ministry of Good News Publishers. Used by permission. All rights reserved."

Scripture taken from the New King James Version® Copyright © 1982 by Thomas Nelson. Used by permission. All rights reserved.

ISBN: 978-1-6642-7319-1 (sc)
ISBN: 978-1-6642-7320-7 (e)

Library of Congress Control Number: 2022913439

Print information available on the last page.

WestBow Press rev. date: 10/14/2022

DEDICATION

This devotional is dedicated to my saintly mother, Stella Mae Mason Parson, who taught me that what God required of me was to live justly, love mercy, and walk humbly with my God. Momma had an intimacy and friendship with Jesus that blessed us all. Having that kind of walk with God has inspired this book and I dedicate it to her memory and legacy. You were right, Momma, what a friend we have in Jesus!

CONTENTS

PART TWO: WALKING WITH GOD
Staying In Step
Devotionals 18-74

PART THREE: STAY CLOSE
Devotionals 75-106

PART FOUR: LIVE IN LOVE

(Devotions 107 – 139 are influenced by Gary Chapman's book, The Five Love Languages)

PART FIVE: THE ENOCH EXPERIENCE
Devotionals 140-158

INTRODUCTION

"And Enoch walked with God: and he was not; for God took him."

— Genesis 5:24 (KJV)

"Enoch walked faithfully with God; then he was no more, because God took him away."

— Genesis 5:24 (NIV)

"Enoch walked steadily with God. And then one day he was simply gone: God took him."

— Genesis 5:24 (MSG)

"He spent his life in fellowship with God, and then he disappeared, because God took him away."

— Genesis 5:24 (GNB)

"He has shown you, O mortal, what is good. And what does the Lord require of you? To act justly and to love mercy and to walk humbly with your God."

— Micah 6:8 (NIV)

There is no greater joy on this earth than the opportunity to walk with God. What did Noah do to earn God's favor? What great feat did Abraham accomplish to get the attention of God? What supernatural thing did Isaac do to have his name called throughout the ages? Why was Job blessed? What was so impressive about little David that he would be chosen? And what was so special about Enoch that he was just taken away? Maybe the answer is in Micah 6:8. Maybe they simply walked with God. I like how the Good News Bible says it, a life in fellowship with God.

This devotional is a journey. Although each lesson can stand on its own, taken together in sequence they will take you on a journey as you learn to walk with God. Each entry has a scripture, an explanation, an application, and an action step at the end. If you will do the things suggested in this devotional each day you read one of them, at the end of this book you will have a deeper, more satisfying, and more intimate walk with God. There are several hundred scriptures in these devotions, so you'll know the Bible better at the end as well. But, more than that, you will have learned so much more about the nature of God, what He expects, and His desires for you.

You will find lots of repetition in this book. Some of the lessons may be identical in their theme. This is on purpose. Repetition is a great teacher and so you will find many of the concepts here presented repeatedly. But that's exactly what walking is-taking the same kind of steps over, and over again. But the more you step, and the more you repeat the steps, the more intimate your relationship with God will be, and the more joyous your walk with Him. And oh, the places you will go!

You will also see in this devotional that every pronoun related to God will be capitalized. This may not be proper English; however, it is done for two reasons. One reason is my adoration and respect for God. I honor Him by capitalizing every pronoun and name that refers to the God of the universe. The other reason is for clarity, so you will know every time the scripture is referring to deity rather than humanity.

This full book is designed to take you through a year of walking with God if you do about three devotionals per week. So, let's get started on the greatest walk you will ever take in your life. It will be an experience; the Enoch experience: how to walk with God!

1   GOD IS MORE THAN CHURCH

The earth is the Lord's, and everything in it, the world, and all who live in it.

– Psalm 24:1 (NIV)

Our God is the Creator of the universe. The earth is His. The world is His. Everyone is His. Everything is His. All are under, not only His command, but also His watchful eye. He is a master planner and an eternal strategist. How sad it is that we have reduced His interests, and our interest in Him, to only the things that pertain to our church service on Sunday morning and our weekly Bible study. Our God is so much bigger than that! When you walk with Him today, as you speak with Him throughout your day, and as you think thoughts toward Him when you rest at night, consider asking Him about things you never thought you could. What are His favorite things? What was He thinking when He created the mountains? What breaks His heart?

You may not believe God talks to people anymore as He did in the Bible. That's okay. When you ask Him questions, He has a way of getting you the answer in a way you can believe. But He would enjoy you just walking and talking with Him and asking the questions. Pray something that is more about Him and less about you. There is so much more to God than you know. He would love to reveal Himself and let you know Him. What a joy!

God is a God you can know. He is a Father you can depend on. He is a friend you can share your life with. He is a companion you can travel this earthly journey with, and there is so much more to Him than church. The Bible is full of people who personally walked with God outside of religious institutions, sacrificial missions, and world-changing assignments. God didn't create us just to put us to work to accomplish some terrestrial tasks. We were created in His image with minds and spirits that have the capacity to know the God of the universe and be in relationship with Him. He has invited us to walk with Him and discover the mysteries of all that He is. Find something interesting to ask Him about today. He is waiting to share life with you. "Now this is eternal life: that they know You, the only true God, and Jesus Christ Whom You have sent" (John 17:3 NIV).

2 GOD IS RELATIONAL

He has shown you, O mortal, what is good. And what does the Lord require of you? To act justly, and to love mercy, and to walk humbly with your God.

— Micah 6:8 (NIV)

God is relational. From His conversations with Adam and Eve in Genesis to the welcoming home of His children in Revelation, the story of the Bible is the story of God's relationship with His creation, humankind. God is clear that His expectation for us is that we stay in relationship with Him.

Micah states God's requirements very simply. Do justly. Love mercy. Walk with Me. Do what is right. Treat others with compassion. Stay in habitual relationship with Me. Share your life with Me. God wants us to share the ups and downs of life with Him. Go with Him through all the good times and the bad. Talk to Him about your work frustrations. Be aware of His presence at weddings, graduations, the births of babies, in hospital rooms, and in the face of death. My favorite hymn is "In the Garden." The song starts out with "I come to the garden alone, while the dew is still on the roses, and the voice I hear falling on my ear, the Son of God discloses … and He walks with me and He talks with me and He tells me I am His own. And the joy we share as we tarry there, none other has ever known." Walk with God.

God is relational, and He longs to be in relationship with you. Daily. For a lifetime. You can truly know Him, His voice, and His plan for your life, all through His Son, Jesus Christ. Take a walk with Him today. Go outside and walk with Him. Talk to Him. Start building a relationship. You may be surprised where this relationship takes you.

Naida M. Parson, Ph.D

3 HABITUAL FELLOWSHIP

Enoch walked [in habitual fellowship] with God after the birth of Methuselah 300 years and had other sons and daughters. So, all the days of Enoch were 365 years. And Enoch walked [in habitual fellowship] with God; and he was not, for God took him [home with Him].

— Genesis 5:22–24 (AMP)

To walk with God means to be in habitual fellowship with Him, to daily interact with Him, and to share life together. It is the Enoch experience we all can have. Because Jesus Christ paid the penalty for our sins, we have been brought back into right relationship with God. Our sins separated us from God, but now we are reconciled. We are back in His good graces. We can all have the experience of walking with God. This devotional is all about how to build and maintain a lifetime of habitual fellowship with God.

What is habitual fellowship? It is being with God daily. It's being constantly aware of His presence. It's listening for His voice throughout the day and calling on Him regularly for your needs and even your wants. It's allowing Him to be your companion and including Him in your daily activities. Enoch walked with God. The Bible doesn't tell us what all that entailed, but as we read the scriptures and examine Bible stories, we know there must have been lots of talking involved. I'm sure there was worship and appreciation. Correction would have been present and many questions asked and answered, both ways. There is no mention here of great tasks, supernatural accomplishments, or worldwide revivals. Just a man walking with God. God apparently liked it so much He continued it to another world.

Enoch had habitual fellowship with God. So can you. Today, include Him in something new in your day by saying a prayer and acknowledging that He is there. That's a great place to start. Then make sure you finish this book. It will show you how to make sure your walk never ends.

4   SEEK HIM OUT

Because of faith Enoch was caught up and transferred to heaven, so that he did not have a glimpse of death; and he was not found, because God had translated him. For even before he was taken to heaven, he received testimony [still on record] that he had pleased and been satisfactory to God. But without faith it is impossible to please and be satisfactory to Him. For whoever would come near to God must [necessarily] believe that God exists and that He is the rewarder of those who earnestly and diligently seek Him [out].

– Hebrews 11:5–6 (AMP)

We don't know much about Enoch from the Bible, except that he prophesied as recorded in Jude 1:14. Although, there is some information out there about him if we look it up, as far as the Bible is concerned, all we know about Enoch is that he walked with God, disappeared one day with God, and that he pleased God. God was totally satisfied with his life. Not because he wrote psalms like David or built a temple like Solomon. Not because he freed slaves like Moses or called fire from heaven like Elijah. He simply walked with God, and God was so pleased with that relationship that He just took Enoch with Him.

After commending Enoch, the next verse in Hebrews says that without faith it is impossible to please God and that to come near to God, you must first believe that God exists and that He rewards those who will seek Him out. Could it be that this verse follows Enoch because Enoch sought God out? God doesn't just want to chase us our whole lives. What He really wants is a people who will seek Him out. God wants us to want to know Him. He would love for us to consider Him so important, so desirable, that we take the time to seek Him out.

Do it today. Don't wait for Him to tap you on your shoulder. Don't wait for the guilt to set in and motivate you to pray so you feel better. You make the first move. Seek Him out. Tell Him you want to know Him. Tell Him you want to be with Him today. Ask Him to show you something new about Him. That would please Him, and it will bless you tremendously.

Naida M. Parson, Ph.D

5 SPEND TIME WITH HIM

As Jesus and His disciples were on their way, He came to a village where a woman named Martha opened her home to Him. She had a sister called Mary, who sat at the Lord's feet listening to what He said. But Martha was distracted by all the preparations that had to be made. She came to Him and asked, "Lord, don't you care that my sister has left me to do the work by myself? Tell her to help me!" "Martha, Martha," the Lord answered, "you are worried and upset about many things, but few things are needed—or indeed only one. Mary has chosen what is better, and it will not be taken away from her."

– Luke 10:38–42 (NIV)

We often measure our dedication to God by how busy we are working for Him. We have been influenced to think the spiritual ones are the ones who work at the church or volunteer there several times a week. We believe the secret to pleasing God is more Bible studies, extra services, attendance at church functions, and of course, monetary offerings. We are so busy doing work for the Lord that we miss quality time with the Lord.

It's kind of like marriage with children. There is a lot of one-to-one intimacy when the marriage starts, but then the kids come, and the mortgage, and the bills, and everything becomes about the kids and the house. Every conversation, all the energy, the time, and the money, become focused on the business of the house and the responsibility of the children. Intimacy is lost, and though all of it is done *for* love, soon you're no longer *in* love. God doesn't want you so busy working for Him, like Martha, that you forget pure, loving time with Him, like Mary.

We all know it's God's will that we become more like Him, as well as become the best versions of ourselves. For that to happen we must experience transformation. Church work doesn't change you. Busy work doesn't change you. Just coming to church doesn't change you. Relationship will change you. Your relationship with God through Jesus Christ will take care of all the dos and don'ts. You will do everything out of love and relationship and that will make all the difference in the world. So today, or as soon as you can this week, schedule some time with God where you are not distracted by anything else. Just try 30 minutes, and then build from there. Guard that time with your life. By the time you finish this book, it will be your life.

6 IT'S AN AMAZING LOVE

"The Lord appeared to us in the past, saying: "I have loved you with an everlasting love; I have drawn you with unfailing kindness."

– Jeremiah 31:3 (NIV)

When you practice walking with God, you will begin to feel drawn to Him every day. Then it grows to a few times a day. Then it begins to happen all throughout the day. You feel a nudge. You feel a pull. Your thoughts drift toward Him. His love draws you. It's an amazing love. Just think of how He loves us past our faults and failures. Past all the disobedient and ungodly things we do right in His face. We use the health, the strength, and the resources He gave us to do the opposite of what pleases Him, even to the point of breaking His heart. And still, He loves. And still, He is kind. And still, He draws us closer. It's an amazing love. It's unconditional in a way that most of us cannot fully comprehend. Human love doesn't seem to work that way. It eventually requires reciprocation to survive. We have seen loving parents give up on children, and lovers who once could not breath without each other, walk away. But the love of God stands stronger than any force in nature when it is reciprocated, and when it is not. When He sends rain, it falls on the just and the unjust.

It's an amazing love and it will begin to draw you more and more. It is everlasting and kind. When we are at our lowest, we can ask the question that must have been in the mind of the lost son whom we call the prodigal, "Who can love me like this?" Your answer is the same as what finally dawned on him. My Father. My Father is the only one who can love me like this! At my lowest. After I have sinned. After I have ignored Him so long. So, I'm drawn to Him. I am drawn to find my way home to my Father. And I will find Him with His arms open and waiting for me. Rejoicing to have me in His presence again. Forgiving me for my absence and my foolishness. Ready to bless me with gifts I do not deserve. It's an amazing love. And it will draw you.

When you feel that nudge today, or when your thoughts drift toward Him, speak to Him. Just say hello. Whisper a praise like "You're wonderful" or "I love You" or "amazing God." While you're driving in your car, just say out loud "You're awesome." While shopping or working, tell Him how much you appreciate the provision He has made for you. And in the morning, or evening, or whenever you have scheduled your quiet time with Him, don't let anything stop you from going. His love is drawing you. It's an amazing love.

Naida M. Parson, Ph.D

7 THERE IS SOMETHING ABOUT THE MORNING

"In the morning, Lord, You hear my voice; in the morning I lay my requests before You and wait expectantly."

– Psalm 5:3 (NIV)

God will welcome time with you any day and any time of day. But there is something about the morning. Starting your day with a quiet moment with God seems to be a favorite of His. David, a man after God's own heart, called on God in the morning. Jesus was known to seek God in the early watches. I think God likes the morning because it shows the priority you put on your time with Him. This is no hard and fast rule but consider all the significant relationships you have. Consider the people you live with and love the most. Would you start your day without at least a "good morning?" Do people who are crazily in love wait until lunchtime to say their first hello of the day? Maybe in your world they do because of schedules and busyness and night shifts. But, for most of us, our thoughts go to the ones we love in the morning.

Here's another reason to start your walk with God in the morning. Satan, the enemy of your soul, would like to have first dibs on your day. He wants to bring worry and stress and bustle. He wants your day to be filled with frustration and dissatisfaction and striving for everything except relationship with God. Think about the thermostat in your house. Whoever gets to it first can set it wherever they want. Soon the atmosphere of the room conforms to where the thermostat is set. Satan wants to beat you to the thermostat of your day. But when you seek God in the morning, when He hears your voice and you set your requests for the day before Him, you have beaten your enemy to the thermostat of your day and now it is set on the things of God.

Consider developing a habit of finding time with God in the morning. Even if it means getting up fifteen minutes earlier to be quiet with Him. Set the time to read, or worship, or listen, or go through a devotional like this. It will enhance the atmosphere of your soul and spirit. It will demonstrate the priority of God in your life. It will make Him smile. It will make your day.

8 GOD, YOU KNOW ME

"You have searched me, Lord, and You know me. You know when I sit and when I rise; You perceive my thoughts from afar. You discern my going out and my lying down; You are familiar with all my ways. Before a word is on my tongue You, Lord, know it completely. You hem me in behind and before, and You lay Your hand upon me. Such knowledge is too wonderful for me, too lofty for me to attain."

– Psalm 139:1-6 (NIV)

Some have said that intimacy means "in-to-me-see." God desires to have an intimate personal relationship with all of His children and no one sees into us like our God! Our Father. Our Creator. He knows our every thought. He watches over our every activity. He is familiar with all of our ways. He knows the way we eat, the way we love, the way we procrastinate, or the way we try to control our environment. We are all as unique as the fingerprint that He gave us. Yet, no matter how complicated, intricate, and unpredictable we may be, He knows us, and He has worked our every action and reaction into the fabric of His will for our lives.

We don't have to have any pretense with God. No need to be phony or attempt to be "presentable" in His presence. David says in this Psalm, "Lord, You know me." I can't fool You. I can't con You. I can't manipulate You with words or seduce You with my deeds. You know me. So, I can come to You raw. Naked, and not ashamed. You love me just like this with all the faults and failures that are in me that no one else can see.

So come to Him today. Just like you are. Have a real conversation about you with the God who truly loves you. And know that when it's over, He will love you the same because He already knew. Walk with Him today. Talk with Him. Have the most real and honest conversation you have ever had. Perhaps this is the only place you truly can.

Naida M. Parson, Ph.D

9   PRACTICE HIS PRESENCE

"Where can I go from Your Spirit? Where can I flee from Your presence? If I go up to the heavens, You are there; if I make my bed in the depths, You are there. If I rise on the wings of the dawn, if I settle on the far side of the sea, even there Your hand will guide me, Your right hand will hold me fast."

– Psalm 139:7-10 (NIV)

"Practice makes perfect," according to a famous quote. If we are going to grow into an extraordinary relationship with God, we must learn to practice being acutely aware of His presence. It is so easy to leave God out of our consciousness. It's easy, and perhaps advantageous to our sinful nature, to forget He is ever present. Someone once said that when we ignore the presence of God, especially when we are committing some sin against Him, at that point, we become atheists. For that moment, we wish that God didn't exist.

We must live in the acute awareness of the presence of God. As we drive in our cars, He is our companion and our safety. As we sleep at night, He is present in our bedrooms guarding our hearts and forming our dreams. As we go about our day, He is present to lead us into truth, to help us accomplish tasks, to bring about successes, and to open our eyes to opportunities to share Him with others. He is present in our low experiences, in the depths, as we go through sickness, or death, or disaster. He is omnipresent. Everywhere, at all times, He is available to talk to, to discuss the major and the minor things in our lives, and to help us make right decisions and stay in step with Him.

Today, practice the presence of God. Keep an open conversation with Him. See Him with spiritual eyes in your home, in your car, on your job, and in your troubles and triumphs. It's rude to ignore someone who is in the room with you. So, talk to Him, laugh with Him, ask Him questions. He is present.

10 EVEN IN DARKNESS ... WALK

"If I say, "Surely the darkness will hide me and the light become night around me," even the darkness will not be dark to You; the night will shine like the day, for darkness is as light to You."

– Psalm 139:11-12 (NIV)

David is simply saying that no matter what, God is present. But when I read this verse, I think about my dark days. Those days when I'm so low, I operate as if God is not present. Those days when my own dark side is out. Sometimes in walking with God, your times with Him will seem to be interrupted by your own darkness. The darkness may come from a sin in your life. The darkness may come from a tragedy or loss. The darkness may come from depression or sickness. Whatever the reason for your dark days, the reality of walking with God is that light and dark are the exact same to Him.

God is so faithful, and so into you, that He is just as present and willing to walk with you in your darkness as He is in your light. This of course makes sense when you have experienced tragedy, sickness, or sadness. He is the One who embraces and sustains you. He is the One who carries you, like in the famous poem we call "Footprints." But what if your darkness is caused by that sin in your life? Sin separates us from God. It is during these times when walking with God seems to be impossible until we repent and get it right.

Still, this scripture says that I can't hide from God, even in my darkness. Yes, sin separated us from God, but Jesus paid the price for our sins and fulfilled the wrath of God over them. In other words, when you commit a sin, that is no longer a reason to separate yourself from God. Don't spend days out of step with God. Just confess the sin and get back in step. I have found that I didn't have to clean up to come into His presence. I could come dirty and let His blood cover and cleanse me. I am able to walk with God because of the righteousness of Jesus Christ. On my best day, on my light days, I am not clean enough to walk with God. Only Jesus is, so I just stand in Him. Today, confess your sins and accept the cleansing power of the blood and never stop walking with Him ... ever.

Naida M. Parson, Ph.D

11 WHEN YOU WERE GOO ... HE KNEW

"For You created my inmost being; You knit me together in my mother's womb. I praise You because I am fearfully and wonderfully made; Your works are wonderful, I know that full well. My frame was not hidden from You when I was made in the secret place, when I was woven together in the depths of the earth. Your eyes saw my unformed body; all the days ordained for me were written in Your book before one of them came to be."

– Psalm 139:13-16 (NIV)

Intimacy. In-to-me-see. God knows you. He really knows you. And He wants you to know Him intimately. You have the opportunity to have intimate relationship with the Almighty God. He saw you when you were goo in your mother's womb and has watched over your form and shape through every season of your life.

There is no need for shame or embarrassment at your failures or faults. He knows you! You can't surprise Him. You can't disappoint Him. You can't shock Him. He knows you! He knew you would fail and fall and falter. He knew you would think and act that way. He knew you would rebel about this and obey about that. He knows what makes you rejoice and what makes you cry. And in all that He knew-your resume and your record-He chose to love you. He chose to save you. He chose to invite you to walk with Him.

So, accept His invitation without fear. Get to know Him. Intimately. Through His word, through experiences, through reading the words of this book. You are about to have a journey of intimacy with the God that knows you, sees you and has chosen YOU.

12 YOU'RE ON HIS MIND

"How precious to me are Your thoughts, God! How vast is the sum of them! Were I to count them, they would outnumber the grains of sand— when I awake, I am still with You."

— Psalm 139:17-18 (NIV)

It's always wonderful to get a card, or a telephone call, or a text message that says, "I was just thinking about you." It's comforting to know that you are on someone's mind. As you develop intimacy with God, it's amazing to know that you are on His mind. He is constantly thinking of you. David, the writer of this psalm, felt that the fact that God thought about him was precious. Of all the things the Creator of the universe has to think about, He thinks about us.

This is wonderful, especially when we read Jeremiah 29:11. "I know the thoughts I think toward you says the Lord. Thoughts of peace and not of evil, to bring you a future and a hope." This word that is translated "thoughts" can also be translated "plans." God's thoughts are His plans. So, when God thinks of me, He is developing great plans for me as well. He is working out my future and ordering all my steps. He is being intentional about me. He is thinking of everything and working it out in advance.

Walking with God means that you both spend lots of time thinking about each other. You are on God's mind and He should be on yours. Think of Him often today. Think of how good He has been to you and how well He takes care of you. Rest in the fact that He has thoughts of you, and as you walk with Him, He reveals His plan for your life. Ask Him to show you just a little of what He has in mind!

Naida M. Parson, Ph.D

13 GOD KNOWS MY HEART

"Search me, God, and know my heart; test me and know my anxious thoughts. See if there is any offensive way in me and lead me in the way everlasting."

– Psalm 139:23-24 (NIV)

In the church tradition where I grew up, there was a saying people used when their behavior was not quite in line with Christian principles. They would say "God knows my heart". I always considered that a scary statement because the truth is, He really does! He is intimate with you. He sees into you. And when your motives aren't right and your sin is just rebellion against Him, He really does know your heart … way better than you do.

David had already written about how well God knew him. So why does David invite God into where He already exists? This Psalm is about relationship. David is saying, "God, let's have a conversation about my heart. Show me what's in it. Show me *me*. Examine me, Lord. Show me my thoughts and correct whatever You find in me that is not upright."

In your time with God today, ask Him to show you things only He knows about you. Ask Him to reveal to you thoughts and feelings that don't fit in the mind of one who walks with God. You may be surprised at what He has already found. There may be good, bad, and ugly. But there will also be grace to forgive and correct, and you will have a greater intimacy because you have shared together what no one else can share. The Bible says that our hearts are deceitful and that we don't know our own heart. But, since our hearts are the essence of who we are, we must allow God to examine, correct, and renew them. That is our task today. Lord, let's have a conversation about my heart.

14 AT THE END OF THE DAY

"By day the Lord directs His love, at night His song is with me— a prayer to the God of my life."

– Psalm 42:8 (NIV)

It's a wonderful thing to wake up next to the one we love each morning, and then to lay down at night with the same person you are devoted to and spend your life with. Whatever happens throughout the day, it is such a comfort to know that at the end of the day you have a place to belong, to relax, and to embrace.

What a joy it is not only to seek God first thing in the morning, but also to have Him be the last person you speak to at night. If you're single this is easy. If you have a marriage and/or children, not so much, but when you make it a priority, you can sneak a minute before the end your day and have a love encounter with God. Thank Him for another day. Ask for forgiveness for any slips along the way. Pray about concerns the day brought. Reflect on your time with Him during the day. Commit to Him anything you're facing the next day. Maybe just say that you're looking forward to meeting Him in the morning for your quiet time. Some may even make the nighttime their main quiet time with God. However you can pull it off, walking with God is enhanced by beginning your day with Him and ending your day with Him.

Bedtime prayer is a tradition for many of us. It is something we learned as children with prayers like "now I lay me down to sleep." For the Christian who is walking with God it can be the sweetest part of the day. Make it a family affair again for all in your household if that's the best way. But a personal, intimate goodnight is relationship building. The psalmist in this scripture considered it having God's song with him during the night. Begin and end your day with Jesus. It will bring peace. It will bring comfort. It will bring intimacy. It will bring His song into your spirit and maybe even sweeter dreams.

Naida M. Parson, Ph.D

15 HELP!

"I lift up my eyes to the mountains— where does my help come from? My help comes from the Lord, the Maker of heaven and earth."

– Psalm 121:1-2 (NIV)

The great thing about walking daily with God is that you are quite aware that He is there when you need some help. Of course, you need His help every day to live and function and do the things you need to do. You need His help to be effective on your job, or to raise your children, or keep your marriage working. You need His help for finances and health and mental stability. But there are days that you need special help … right now help. You need help when things are overwhelming, and you feel like you don't have the wherewithal to maneuver your current situation. Life can get to the point that you feel at wits end. You feel like you're losing the battle. You feel you have nothing left to offer a difficult situation.

This is where David was in this psalm. There are lots of interpretations of this verse, but the one I like is that David, being a man of war, was in a situation where the battle was too much for him and it began to feel like he was losing. During those times, the cavalry would hopefully come over the hill tops to help. Those extra troops would show up at the right time to take on the battle. But this time, David looked to the mountains and hills and no help was coming. He asked the question- where does my help come from?

He realized that his help came from the Lord. The Lord would help him in this battle. The Lord would take over when he was overwhelmed by the battle. Whatever it is you are facing today, realize that walking with God means that He is your ever-present help. Ask Him to help you today. Realize, all day long, that He is your help through the Holy Spirit. Notice the moments where you feel His help and say "thank You" when you do. You are not in this alone. Stop trying to live life, battle life, and handle life alone. You are walking with God. He is right there. Ask Him for His help.

16 ALREADY MESSED UP?

"If we claim to have fellowship with Him and yet walk in the darkness, we lie and do not live out the truth. But if we walk in the light, as He is in the light, we have fellowship with one another, and the blood of Jesus, His Son, purifies us from all sin. If we claim to be without sin, we deceive ourselves and the truth is not in us. If we confess our sins, He is faithful and just and will forgive us our sins and purify us from all unrighteousness."

— 1 John 1:6-9 (NIV)

Even though we are near the beginning of this devotional walk with God, I'm sure most folks reading this book have already messed up. You missed some days. You put the walk aside. You have gotten out of step. You have sinned. You have slipped back into your default settings, meaning you have gone back to some of your old bad habits. It could be something as bad as a major sin-you know, one of the big ones like drugs or abusiveness or sexual immorality. Or it may be one of the small ones like procrastination, missing your prayer time, or eating too much of that sinfully good food.

But sin is sin. There are no levels to it. All unrighteousness is sin. And chances are you have sinned by now. The Bible says that if we claim to be in relationship with God, but still walk in darkness we aren't truthful. This isn't about the slip ups we have and repent for. We've already talked about that kind of darkness. But we can't stay in a state of willful unrepentant sin and say we are in fellowship with God. There is a way to get back on track and stay in the light. There is a way to get back to walking with God.

Even if there is a longstanding rebellion in your life, if you confess your sin, He is faithful and just to forgive you. If you have gotten off track, or have committed any kind of sin, it is not supposed to stop your walk with God. You just confess it, and He forgives it, and the relationship continues! Why is that just? Because Jesus has already paid for the sin. To make you pay for it would be like double jeopardy in court. You can't be convicted and punished for the same crime twice. Jesus took your crime and your punishment. So, justice has been served!

Not only will He forgive, but He will cleanse you from whatever you did wrong and get it out of your life for good. So, if you have faltered, confess it, and keep walking. If you have not, remember this lesson in case you need it later. Better yet, share it with someone who needs it today.

Naida M. Parson, Ph.D

17 PRAYER FOR RELATIONSHIP SAKE

"The Lord would speak to Moses face to face, as one speaks to a friend. Then Moses would return to the camp, but his young aide Joshua, son of Nun, did not leave the tent. Moses said to the Lord, "You have been telling me, 'Lead these people,' but You have not let me know whom You will send with me. You have said, 'I know you by name and you have found favor with Me.' If You are pleased with me, teach me Your ways so I may know You and continue to find favor with You. Remember that this nation is Your people." The Lord replied, "My presence will go with you, and I will give you rest." Then Moses said to Him, "If Your presence does not go with us, do not send us up from here.

And the Lord said to Moses, "I will do the very thing you have asked, because I am pleased with you and I know you by name."

– Exodus 33:11-15, 17 (NIV)

There is a reason people don't pray much. Sometimes people aren't great fans of prayer because they are not convinced prayer works. God does not always do what we want done, the way we want it done, in the time we think we need it done. So why pray about it? Why come all the way down to the church for corporate prayer? Why get up before the birds in the morning for this ineffective prayer? Why not just tell God what you need on the fly and hope He does it?

I admit I used to think this way and prayer was not very central in my personal life. After I got through apologizing for my raggedy self, I actually felt worse than I did before prayer. But, now I have a better revelation! The reason people don't pray much is because we think prayer is about asking and then getting an answer of yes, or no, or wait. That is called supplication and is only one aspect of prayer. PRAYER IS ABOUT BUILDING A LOVING INTIMATE RELATIONSHIP WITH GOD. Moses talked to God face to face like you would a friend. He and God had conversations like "You've been telling me this ... but what about that? "Well, Moses, how about I do this?" "Okay Lord, well, show me this." "Okay I can do that, but like this ... ". Just friends talking one on one. Moses didn't literally see His face, but the conversation was intimate like friends talking face to face.

We don't pray just to get some stuff or to get some problems solved. The best use of prayer is for the sake of relationship. We pray to build relationship through quality time and communication. God wants to hear your voice and He wants you to know His. You get close in prayer. You get intimate in prayer. He makes you laugh. He tells you secrets. He opens your eyes. He straightens out your thinking. He comforts. He cheers you up. He stabilizes your emotions. He encourages. He corrects and convicts. He instructs and affirms. And you get to pour out your heart, share, question, worship. So, when you pray today, let your motive and expectation be different. Prayer is more than you think. It's more than getting blessed. It's more than gaining power. It's relationship …

18 STAYING IN STEP

"The Lord makes firm the steps of the one who delights in Him; though he may stumble, he will not fall, for the Lord upholds him with His hand."

– Psalm 37:23-24 (NIV)

Walking with God means to stay in step with Him every day. God has already walked out the steps of your life. He has made them firm and sure. He knows the way He wants you to go to get to the destination He has preordained. "The steps of the righteous are ordered by the Lord and He delights in his way" is another translation of this scripture. In English, when we use the word "ordered," it can mean to dictate, like ordering a meal, or it can mean arranging, like putting things in a particular sequence. This may not be the most accurate translation, but it certainly is true. God has not only dictated what steps we make, but He also arranges the sequence of them … IF we walk with Him, acknowledge Him, and obey His direction.

Staying in step with God means moving in obedience with His instructions daily. If He asks you to do something and you do something else, you are out of step. If He moves on you to pray and you read instead, you are out of step. If He leads you to go to college and you opt to go on a mission, even though it's great work that would normally please Him, you are out of step because it is not according to what God has ordered. Walking with God is the daily challenge of staying in step with Him in everything you do. He may tell you something as simple as what to eat for your health, or something as serious as move to another city. He may need you to be the answer to someone's prayer that day and so He places someone on your heart to call. Whatever He has ordered for you today, your job is to move in that direction and make that step.

Walk with Him today. Listen for His instruction. Feel for His nudge or impression on your heart. Move where He moves. Stop when and where He stops. Get acquainted with however He speaks to you through the word, or your spirit, or a song. That's what makes daily prayer and quiet time with Him so important. It isn't easy. It is a challenge. But if you stay in step, He will take you places you never dreamed of!

19 ACCEPTED

"Having predestinated us unto the adoption of children by Jesus Christ to Himself, according to the good pleasure of His will, To the praise of the glory of His grace, wherein He hath made us accepted in the Beloved."

– Ephesians 1:5-6 (KJV)

Our walk with God should be enjoyable, intimate, and loving. Some days that is hard for us to experience because we are so discouraged by our faults and failures. Sin is a separator. We know God hates it although He never stops loving us. So, when we come into His presence, we sometimes are more aware of our ugliness than we are of His undying love for us and the fact that we are "accepted in the Beloved."

Enjoying our time with God is rejoicing in the fact that we have been accepted. So much of our lives as human beings is all about being accepted. We have been made to be relational, so being accepted is a great motivator. It affirms us. On the other hand, being rejected is one of life's most hurtful experiences. In Jesus Christ we are accepted by the God of the Universe!

Whatever wrong you have done, and will ever do, has already been dealt with and put away by what Jesus did on the cross. You can come and spend time with God every day knowing that you are eternally accepted. He is already proud of you. He is always glad to see you. His arms are always open. You were predestined to be adopted, and you are accepted as a full child into this family. Nothing you do, or fail to do, will change that when you are in Christ Jesus. It's good to be accepted. This is your place. This is your home. In the presence of God is where you belong. So come to your Father today and just spend time talking to Him. You are accepted here. Always. Forever.

Naida M. Parson, Ph.D

20 GETTING TO KNOW HIM

"But whatever were gains to me I now consider loss for the sake of Christ. What is more, I consider everything a loss because of the surpassing worth of knowing Christ Jesus my Lord, for whose sake I have lost all things. I consider them garbage, that I may gain Christ and be found in Him, not having a righteousness of my own that comes from the law, but that which is through faith in Christ—the righteousness that comes from God on the basis of faith. I want to know Christ—yes, to know the power of His resurrection and participation in His sufferings, becoming like Him in His death, and so, somehow, attaining to the resurrection from the dead."

– Philippians 3:7-11 (NIV)

Paul stated that everything else in life is considered garbage compared to how valuable it is to have an intimate relationship with Jesus Christ. I love the verse where he simply says, "I want to KNOW Christ." Most of the time, when the Bible uses the word "know," it's talking about intimate knowledge. It's talking about relationship. Jesus gave us the indication that when we get to heaven the thing that will matter most is that we know Him … not things we did, or great feats we accomplished. He wants relationship.

So how do we go about developing relationship in our daily walk with God? You build relationship through quality time and communication. We are in the image of God, and so just like we build relationship with each other, we must spend time with Him. It needs to be quality time. That means not giving Him the leftovers or the arbitrary in between. You know, in between commercials, in between lights, in between appointments, or texts, or checking in on Facebook. Those times are okay too, but there are times you need to spend true intimate moments with Him.

Pick a time daily that is just HIS time and then use that time to communicate with Him. Don't just use the time to rant about your issues, your concerns, or your day. Use the time to share your heart and listen as He shares His heart with you. Just keep practicing it. You will get to where you know when He is speaking to you. It may be through a devotional like this, or it may be through the Bible, or a song, or a recorded sermon. But then, more and more, He speaks to you through your own spirit from His Holy Spirit that lives in you. If this is your quality time right now, just sit back and ask Him to share something special with you. The more you talk, the more your relationship builds, until it is the greatest and strongest thing in your life.

21 TALK TO HIM

"Hear my voice when I call, Lord; be merciful to me and answer me. My heart says of you, "Seek His face!" Your face, Lord, I will seek."

– Psalms 27:7-8 (NIV)

God wants to hear your voice and He wants you to hear His. There is nothing wrong with corporate prayer (prayer in a group) where someone leads the prayer. It is powerful and necessary. There is nothing wrong with prayers from a prayer book, or recordings of prayer. Sometimes they help us to say what we want to say and develop the words of prayer. But when it comes to walking with God, He wants to hear your voice.

David, in his intimate relationship with God, asked God to hear his voice when he called on Him. When we are in trouble, or confused, or hurting, it is good to know that God is listening and ready to respond. David asked God to be merciful and answer him. Walking with God means talking to Him and learning how to know when He is talking to you. That is how you get to know Him. David said that his heart tells him to seek the face of God. Our talks with God must go beyond asking Him to do things for us. Just asking God for things is more like seeking His hand. But walking with God is about seeking His face. Walking with God is having reciprocal conversation. He will answer you.

God wants to hear your voice every day. It doesn't matter how you say it. It doesn't have to sound like anyone else's prayer. It doesn't have to be eloquent or even coherent. God is your Father. When a toddler says "wa wa," a parent knows that means water. They don't request the toddler to say, "mother and father, may I have some water, please?" By the time children talk that well, they can get their own water! Just talk to Him in your voice. He is listening. He is waiting. He is excited about it. And He will talk back to you in many ways until you know His voice for sure. Jesus said, "My sheep know My voice." Keep at it. Start now. Do it today. Talk to Him and expect an answer.

Naida M. Parson, Ph.D

22 COME CLOSER

"Come near to God and He will come near to you."

– James 4:8a (NIV)

Earlier, in James chapter 4, James is talking about prayer and our motives for praying. He says that we want things, but don't get them because we don't ask for them. Or, if we ask for them, we ask for the wrong reasons. Then after giving a few more observations, including that God is jealous for the part of us that belongs exclusively to Him, he drops this verse in; "Come close to God and He will come close to you."

You get close to God in prayer. You draw close to Him there. Many people only use prayer for requests and prayer is for that as well. Some only use prayer for help in an emergency or crisis. Some only pray at church, or to bless their food. But, throughout this devotional, we will repeat this over and over again because it is central to walking with God. Prayer is for the purpose of relationship. It is how we draw close to God.

My mother taught me this song as a little girl; "What a friend we have in Jesus, all our sins and griefs to bear. What a privilege to carry everything to God in prayer … can you find a friend so faithful who will all our sorrows share? … take it to the Lord in prayer." Jesus was her friend. They were close. She walked with Him like Enoch did. She was a woman of prayer. Come closer to God today. When you pray, tell Him something you would only tell your closest friend. Better yet, tell Him something you wouldn't dare tell your closest friend. He knows anyway. Talking it over will make you closer.

23 FRIENDS

"As the Father has loved me, so have I loved you. Now remain in My love ... I no longer call you servants because a servant does not know his master's business. Instead, I have called you friends, for everything that I learned from My Father I have made known to you."

– John 15:9, 15 (NIV)

Walking daily with God should produce an intimacy with Him. Jesus compares His relationship with the Father with His desired relationship with us. He accomplished that with the disciples. After walking with Him, talking to Him, experiencing life with Him, and being taught by Him, He could say of their relationship that as the Father loved Him, that is how He has loved His disciples. Then He asks them to stay in love with Him ... to remain in His love.

The only way we can have that same experience with the Father and the Son is through our daily and continuous prayer. You get intimate in prayer. It is the only way we can walk with Him, talk to Him, experience life with Him, and be taught by Him. Jesus is not here in the flesh to take a walk with, but we can go to the park and walk with Him by holding a conversation as we would if He were right there. Because guess what? He is! We can go on a drive and ask Him about a subject as if He were sitting in the seat next to you. Because, you guessed it, He is!

Practice this today. Begin developing your intimacy through prayer. Tell Him whatever you want to and ask Him things you always wanted to know. He said we are not servants because a servant wouldn't get certain information out of a Master. But you are His intimate friend. Walk and talk with Him today. Take a drive and talk about the scenery. Ask Him why He likes trees and what the mountains are about. Ask Him what bothers Him and what brings Him joy. You may be surprised at what comes to your heart as you enjoy a deeper intimacy.

Naida M. Parson, Ph.D

24 HE MAKES ME LAUGH

"Sarah said, "God has brought me laughter, and everyone who hears about this will laugh with me.""

– Genesis 21:6 (NIV)

This may sound strange to some of you reading this devotional, and I hesitated to write this one because so many respected Christian teachers don't believe God speaks to us as daily and as intimately as I do. But I have to be true to my own experience. Maybe because I spent most of my life single, or maybe because, like the beloved John, King David, Mary of Bethany, Mary Magdalene, and the Apostle Paul, I wanted a more intimate relationship with Him than people who have a fuller life would care for or seek out. But here goes. He makes me laugh.

Like Sarah in our scripture, there are times God either intervenes with a miracle, or shares with you a truth that makes you laugh out loud. It could be an interesting way He worked something out that you prayed about. Maybe you couldn't see a way for it to work out. And then, He finds the most creative, or the most obvious, or the most gracious way to answer that prayer, or solve that problem, and the sheer joy of watching Him work makes you laugh. Or, it could be a conversation you're having with Him, especially when it's about you, that He points out something, or says something to your heart, or sends you to the right scripture at the right time. It seems so coordinated, or so true, that it makes you laugh.

God has a wonderful sense of humor. If you don't believe that, look at some of the things He created, like human beings and our interesting parts! Sarah was waiting for a miracle child. She lost faith several times, but she never lost hope. When God promised her a child when she was nearly ninety, she laughed out of sarcasm. But when she held that child at ninety, she laughed out of pure joy. The joke was on her. God waited until it was, not too late, but way too late to do something as outlandish as this. And it made her laugh. Laughter is good for any relationship. If you need some joy and a good chuckle every now and then, keep walking and talking with God. He just might make you laugh, today.

25 SECRETS

"Call to Me and I will answer you and will tell you great and hidden things that you have not known."

– Jeremiah 33:3 (ESV)

One of the wonderful things about walking with God is that He tells you secrets. He asks Jeremiah to call to Him and declares that He will answer him. Jeremiah had the type of relationship with God where they would hold conversations and God would tell him things He had not told anyone before. Great and hidden things. Secrets. Jesus told His disciples that He was no longer going to call them servants because a servant had no idea what his master was up to. But He called them His friends because He told them … secrets.

I believe we can have as close of a relationship with God as we would like to. For those who would draw near to Him and walk with Him, He has great and hidden things to tell you about. Why does that matter? What is the big deal? Well, isn't that what intimacy is all about? What makes you intimate with a person is that you know things about them no one else knows. And they know things about you that you have hidden from your casual acquaintances. You are vulnerable with that person because you have put parts of yourself out there to them that you would never put out to the world. And it makes you closer. You know at that point that you are loved for the real you.

God already knows you that way. He created you and He even knows your thoughts before you think them. But He wants a two-way relationship. He wants you to know Him, too. He wants to tell you things you would have had no idea about if it were not for the intimacy you have with Him. Oh, it may not be anything that He has never shared with anyone in the world. That would be scary and probably how new religions start when someone believes that. But it would be things that no one else could tell you or reveal to you. It could be a burden He has in the world that He wants to share with His friend so you can pray or act on it. Bottom line … it will make you closer. So, call on Him and He will answer and tell you great and hidden things! Call Him now.

Naida M. Parson, Ph.D

26 BLIND SPOTS

"Then Job replied to the Lord: "I know that You can do all things; no purpose of Yours can be thwarted. You asked, 'Who is this that obscures My plans without knowledge?' Surely, I spoke of things I did not understand, things too wonderful for me to know. "You said, 'Listen now, and I will speak; I will question you, and you shall answer Me.' My ears had heard of You but now, my eyes have seen You."

– Job 42:1-5 (NIV)

We all have blinds spots in our lives. There are areas that we do not see clearly and some we don't see at all. We may have a totally different view of ourselves than what others see. Or, we may have a perspective on an issue or problem that is far from reality. When we have a faulty perception, we come to wrong conclusions. That leads to missteps and mistakes all because we just did not see it that way. When you walk daily with God, He opens your eyes to things you did not know or did not understand.

Job was a man who walked with God. Yet, when it was his time to be tested, he had some faulty perceptions of God. He was angry with God and accused Him of unfair treatment. He felt like if he could just talk to God directly, he would state his case and help God see his point of view. God was much obliged to talk to Job directly. He let Job know that his finite knowledge was no match for God's omniscient wisdom. God knows everything, created everything, and controls everything. Job knew little, created nothing, and controlled absolutely nothing. After Job's talk with God, he could see. His eyes were open. He understood now that God was God alone, and that his life was still in God's hands.

When you come to God with your questions and confusions and conflicts, He is not intimidated, nor put off by your inquiries. He wants you to see things from His perspective. He wants you to know Him, know yourself, and know what to do with your life. God is a God of truth, and He delights in bringing light to everything that has us in the dark. In your quiet times with God, He will open your eyes to great and wonderful things, and some not so wonderful things, too! In your prayer today, ask Him about something you need to see more clearly. If you can't think of anything, ask Him to reveal something about you that you may not be aware of. You can also ask Him to reveal more of Himself so you can know Him in a way you haven't known Him before.

27 THINKING STRAIGHT

"Do not be anxious about anything, but in every situation, by prayer and petition, with thanksgiving, present your requests to God. And the peace of God, which transcends all understanding, will guard your hearts and your minds in Christ Jesus. Finally, brothers and sisters, whatever is true, whatever is noble, whatever is right, whatever is pure, whatever is lovely, whatever is admirable—if anything is excellent or praiseworthy— think about such things."

– Philippians 4:6-8 (NIV)

When you walk with God and spend time with Him in prayer, He straightens out your thinking. Most of what the enemy (the devil and the demons assigned to you) does is simply a mental attack. He speaks words of anxiety and fear and doubt to us, and we tend to ponder on his words until we begin to believe them ourselves. We hear the words of our enemy everywhere during our day. The negativity may come through our families and friends. It may come through the television or movies. It may come from our own patterns of thinking that have developed through the years. So, we are anxious and doubtful of God. This leads to depression and sadness at times.

This is not the way God wants His children to live. It is His will that we have joy and peace in our lives. So instead of being anxious, He tells us in His word to pray. Ask Him for what you need, and be thankful, believing in faith that He will handle every issue. Then He says to think on the right things. After you pray, don't go back to that wrong pattern of thinking. Instead, use prayer to straighten out your thoughts.

Think on things that are true. Most of what we think about that sends us into a negative emotional place is not even true. Then the Bible says to think on what is noble, right, pure, lovely, and admirable. Take a few minutes in your devotional time today and look up all those words. Practice today, and all this week, to think on these things. In your time with God, He will help you by speaking to your heart what His truth is over what your thoughts have been. Let Him straighten out your thinking today and every day.

Naida M. Parson, Ph.D

28 BREATHE AGAIN

"Comfort, comfort My people, says your God. Speak tenderly to Jerusalem and proclaim to her that her hard service has been completed, that her sin has been paid for, that she has received from the Lord's hand double for all her sins."

– Isaiah 40:1-2 (NIV)

God has a way to comfort His people when trouble comes. Through your prayer and constant communication with Him, He comforts. In this scripture, His people had been warned of the punishment to come because of their disobedience. For several chapters, the Prophet Isaiah lays out their sins and their impending consequences. Then, in the 40th chapter, everything changes. God begins to comfort His people.

"Comfort", in the original language, can be translated "breathe again." When we are in trouble, we literally hold our breath. That's why when the trouble passes, we let out a deep sigh of relief. Sometimes we don't even realize that we have stopped breathing. So, whatever your stressors are, whether you caused them or whether they are just part of life on planet earth, when you communicate and walk with God, He will comfort you. He will speak to you. He will show you the truth and give you a way out.

So today, take all your cares to Him. Don't get caught up in worrying about it. Don't get stuck hurting or grieving. You have access to the God of all comfort! He is saying to you that He has your world under control, and you can breathe again. You have been waiting to exhale. You have been waiting for the job to come through, or the marriage to improve, or the kids to straighten out, or for that issue to resolve. But God will comfort you right now if you come to Him and let Him have it. He comforts. Breathe.

29 CHEER UP

"You make known to me the path of life; You will fill me with joy in Your presence, with eternal pleasures at Your right hand."

— Psalm 16:11 (NIV)

Spending time in the presence of God will bring you joy. He cheers you up. As you talk with Him and walk with Him, He has a way of making everything better. God has a light side ... a sense of humor even. He shows you the brighter side of things and how every circumstance of your life has worked out for your good.

When the cares of life have you down and worried, He reminds you of His love, His care, and His ability to work miracles on your behalf. He reminds you of the many times before that He has turned situations totally around. He assures you of victory. He affirms that He is for you. He may point you to a promise in His word. He may bring back a memory of a time where the outcome was all but lost had He not intervened, interrupted, or intercepted.

There is great joy in the presence of an Almighty God who loves you, is for you, and has the power to transform anything. At any time and for any reason, God can turn your day completely around. Take today and enjoy His presence. Ask Him for what you need. Listen for His answer. Take your stress to Him. Leave your worries at His feet. On your worst day, He cheers you up like no one else can.

Naida M. Parson, Ph.D

30 PERFECT PEACE

"You will keep in perfect peace those whose minds are steadfast, because they trust in You."

— Isaiah 26:3 (NIV)

Throughout our lives we face challenges that can keep us on an emotional roller coaster. The world offers many remedies from alcohol, to tranquilizers, to Marijuana, to massage. Our minds are filled with our issues, problems, challenges, and situations. We constantly keep our minds going, trying to figure out how we can fix things, control things, and improve our lives. Everyone is simply trying to make it through traumas, stressors, and pressures. There is a better way.

Your time with God has the side effect of stabilizing your emotions. The word declares that God will keep us in a state of perfect peace when our minds are steadfast on Him and His word. We are at peace because we trust Him. Our hope is not in the economy, or in technology, or in political leadership. Our hope is not even in ourselves or our family and friends. We trust that God is for us and will work everything out in our favor.

Today is a good day to keep your mind and heart focused on God. Talk to Him about every issue and challenge. Simply tell Him what you need, ask Him for His guidance, discuss with Him every decision, and read and repeat His promises. Read about what He has done for others. Meditate on His goodness and every time He has come through for you. Then ask Him for that peace that He promised. His peace. His perfect peace. Peace that is full and complete. Feel the stability rest in your emotional life and when you are challenged again … repeat. Try it today.

31 ENCOURAGEMENT FOR TOUGH DAYS

"David was greatly distressed because the men were talking of stoning him; each one was bitter in spirit because of his sons and daughters. But David found strength in the Lord his God."

— 1 Samuel 30:6 (NIV)

Has life ever hit you so hard that it takes your strength and courage? If it hasn't, it will. During those times, having a personal walk with God is the glue that holds you together. When you come to Him in the midst of challenges and hard circumstances, He gives you strength. He talks you through it. He encourages.

In this scripture, David has had his entire town burned with fire and all the women and children were captured by his enemies. The fighting men who had been out to war with him were devastated and angry and decided to kill their leader. David was hurting too, but he knew his Friend, the God of Heaven, could help him. He remembered their relationship and the things they had been through and conquered together. The King James version of the Bible says, "but David encouraged himself in the Lord, his God". He found strength in God and God reversed all the enemy had done.

When life hits you hard, your strength and encouragement comes from your daily walk with God. You remember all the things the two of you have been through and conquered together. If you don't have those experiences, just keep walking with God, and you will. Talk to Him today about your life and history. He will show you how much was you, and how much was Him, so on those tough days, you can be encouraged and strengthened. Your God can, and will, reverse everything your enemy has done. As you talk with God today, write down your past victories so you can use them to encourage yourself when tough days come. Your victories come from walking with God.

32 PLAN TO BE BETTER

"Have mercy on me, O God, according to Your unfailing love; according to Your great compassion blot out my transgressions. Wash away all my iniquity and cleanse me from my sin. For I know my transgressions, and my sin is always before me. Against You, You only, have I sinned and done what is evil in Your sight; so, You are right in Your verdict and justified when You judge."

– Psalm 51:1-4 (NIV)

I wish we always did the right thing. I wish that, once we start walking with God, we kept Him as our main priority. I wish we always did the things that please Him. But we don't. We mess up. We get off track. We sin. And we aren't always honest with ourselves about what we did, or even why we did it. I am so grateful that there is so much grace in this walk with God. When we don't get it right, we can still go to Him, and He corrects and convicts.

Even when we don't know that we are on the wrong track, He lets us know. Before David wrote this prayer into a psalm, David had sinned and didn't even seem to realize how far he had drifted from God. But, because they had relationship, God was not willing to end their beautiful walk together, though what David did was pretty bad. He had committed adultery and arranged to have a man killed.

God came to David with corrections and David's heart responded with conviction. God returned to David and David returned to God. He admitted his sin and asked to be forgiven and cleansed. Though God didn't take away all the consequences, He did restore their relationship. They walked together for the rest of David's life, and they are still together today. You will falter and fail in this life and God will be gracious enough to bring correction and conviction. He will forgive. He will cleanse. And you will continue to walk together. So, pray to Him today and let Him point out to you the changes you need to make and the places you have gone wrong. Ask for forgiveness and a plan to be better. It's part of the walk. It's part of the experience.

33 GOD CHOICES

"Trust in the Lord with all your heart and lean not on your own understanding; in all your ways submit to Him, and He will make your paths straight."

— Proverbs 3:5-6 (NIV)

Life is complicated. We do not always know what to choose. We seldom know ourselves well enough to know what is right for us. And, on top of that, having to make decisions about what's best for our children, our spouses, our job, or our church. No matter how well read and how well studied we are, there will always be very little we know for sure. Yet, God has given us this earth to have dominion over and He has given us responsibilities. He is holding us accountable for what we do in this world.

And so, He walks with us. It's wonderful to know that we don't have to know because He knows. We don't have to lean to our own understanding because He instructs and affirms what is right when we spend time with Him in prayer. He will direct us. How does this work? When you have a decision to make you bring it to Him first. He has a way of letting you know, either through a strong impression in your spirit, or through a scripture or sermon. Sometimes it will be through wise counsel that identifies strongly with your spirit, or through God sending someone with the answer. He can speak to you so plainly you will know it is Him. And when you are out of step with Him, He makes sure you know that as well. Trust Him with all your heart. Don't worry about making good choices. Make God choices.

It's hard for a Christian walking with God to make a life devastating mistake. He will direct your path and affirm the right way to go. God is for you and wants you to do the right thing every time. So, ask Him today about everything you are concerned about. Don't take a step without Him. Acknowledge Him in everything you do, and He will make your paths straight. And then, have the confidence in Him to know that whatever the outcome, He is in it, and it will turn out in your favor.

Naida M. Parson, Ph.D

34 THE PRIVILEGE OF PRAYER

"In her deep anguish Hannah prayed to the Lord, weeping bitterly. And she made a vow, saying, "Lord Almighty, if You will only look on Your servant's misery and remember me, and not forget Your servant but give her a son, then I will give him to the Lord for all the days of his life, and no razor will ever be used on his head." As she kept on praying to the Lord, Eli observed her mouth. Hannah was praying in her heart, and her lips were moving but her voice was not heard. Eli thought she was drunk and said to her, "How long are you going to stay drunk? Put away your wine." "Not so, my lord," Hannah replied, "I am a woman who is deeply troubled. I have not been drinking wine or beer; I was pouring out my soul to the Lord. Do not take your servant for a wicked woman; I have been praying here out of my great anguish and grief." Eli answered, "Go in peace, and may the God of Israel grant you what you have asked of Him.""

— 1 Samuel 1:10-17 (NIV)

Just think of what a privilege it is to be allowed to pray. You get to have an audience with the God of the universe who is almighty, all knowing and completely holy. You get to speak to Him directly and you get to pour out your heart, share your concerns, question what He has allowed in your life, and worship Him in love and truth. What an honor and a privilege.

Here in these scriptures, Hannah had a situation that caused her intense pain. She was loved, but she had not been able to have a child for her husband. And the woman who did have children would not let her forget it. But Hannah walked with God. She could come to Him with her concern and pour out her soul to Him. She knew that she had access to the God who could change her situation. Even though there were priests in those days who went to God for the people, Hannah was able to speak to God herself. The answer came through her priest, but the prayer came through the anguish of her soul.

God is waiting and willing to hear the very pouring out of your soul, too. Some say you should never question God. I suppose they feel it is disrespectful and untrusting in some way. But we are in a relationship with Him, and people in relationship sometimes need say whatever is on their mind and know that it is a safe place to share. And what a Person to share with! The One Who can actually do something about it. Pour your heart out to Him today. Ask Him questions. Ask Him to fix it for you. He is your God, and He is for you.

35 PRAYER IS MORE THAN YOU THINK

"So now, go. I am sending you to Pharaoh to bring My people the Israelites out of Egypt." But Moses said to God, "Who am I that I should go to Pharaoh and bring the Israelites out of Egypt?" And God said, "I will be with you. And this will be the sign to you that it is I who have sent you: When you have brought the people out of Egypt, you will worship God on this mountain." Moses said to God, "Suppose I go to the Israelites and say to them, 'The God of your fathers has sent me to you,' and they ask me, 'What is His name?' Then what shall I tell them?" God said to Moses, "I Am Who I Am. This is what you are to say to the Israelites: 'I Am has sent me to you.'"

– Exodus 3:10-14 (NIV)

Prayer is more than you think. It's more than getting blessed. It's more than gaining power. It's more than asking God to do things for you or solve your problems. It's more than begging for forgiveness, or praying for a brother, or sister, in need. Prayer is more than praising God, worshipping Him, or giving thanks. Prayer is more than you think. It's relationship.

Moses had a huge job to do for God. But starting off, it was a God he didn't know very well. God is relational. He is more interested in you than He is in any task that He asks you to do. Ultimately, He wants you to know Him. He wants relationship with you. And like any relationship the best way to know each other, feel each other, understand each other, and love on each other is through talking it out. Prayer has lots of purposes, but don't forget that one of them (perhaps the most important one of them) is relationship. The Bible says that God talked to Moses face to face as one speaks to a friend. God wanted Moses to know Who He was. He revealed to Moses a side of Himself no one had ever known before. He wanted Moses to know that He, the Great I Am, was going with him, and that was the most important thing.

God is no respecter of persons, and His personality has not changed. He is still relational. He is still seeking those who want to know Him and be His friend. So, in your prayer time today, talk to your friend. Not to get Him to do anything for you, but to learn more about Him and how to be in relationship with Him. That is what walking with Him is all about. Ask Him what He thinks about. Ask Him what He likes. Ask Him what breaks His heart and what makes His heart glad. Because of Jesus Christ you can come boldly to His throne and talk to Him face to face, just about you and Him. Prayer is more than what you think.

Naida M. Parson, Ph.D

36 PRAY TO OBEY

""Be strong and very courageous. Be careful to obey all the law My servant Moses gave you; do not turn from it to the right or to the left, that you may be successful wherever you go. Keep this Book of the Law always on your lips; meditate on it day and night, so that you may be careful to do everything written in it. Then you will be prosperous and successful."

– Joshua 1:7-8 (NIV)

The key to walking with God is staying in step with Him. This means that you go where He goes, that you stop when He stops, and that you change direction only if He changes direction. In plain terms, walking with God means that you obey Him. When you are in prayer, communicating with God, you will often get specific instructions. Then, as you walk it out, you will feel the Holy Spirit nudging you when you are getting ready to make a decision, or engage in a behavior, that is not in line with the path God has preordained for you. God has a plan and a specific direction for your life. For EVERY area of your life. Staying in step with Him means that you submit your will to Him in everything you do.

In our scripture today, Joshua has been called to take over the leadership of Israel from Moses. It will be his task to take the people into the Promised Land. God wanted him to be successful. God wanted to walk with him and be with him just as He had been with Moses. But the essential habit Joshua would need for his success was to do exactly what God said to do. To walk step by step with Him. God says, "do not turn from it to the right or to the left." He had said to him earlier that He would give him every place where he set his foot! That can only happen if we carefully obey where God tells us to put our feet. There are blessings God already has for you, but you must be in the right place to get them.

Being in fellowship with God means walking out the steps He is guiding you to make. Step by step. Day by day. Hour by hour, you stay sensitive to the Guide living inside of you also known as the Holy Spirit. If it doesn't feel right inside you, stop and pray, and question if this is the right step. You pray to obey. If the decision, or the behavior, comes with a peace inside and it is in line with the scriptures, then you take that step. Today, pray with the expressed intention to obey what you hear and tune into the Spirit guiding you from the inside. If you truly belong to God, you have His Spirit in you and with you. Learn and practice how to listen to your inward Guide. Staying in step with God depends on it.

37 TRUST THE TRACKS

"I make known the end from the beginning, from ancient times, what is still to come. I say, 'My purpose will stand, and I will do all that I please.'"

– Isaiah 46:10 (NIV)

"In Him we were also chosen, having been predestined according to the plan of Him who works out everything in conformity with the purpose of His will,"

– Ephesians 1:11 (NIV)

"For we are God's handiwork, created in Christ Jesus to do good works, which God prepared in advance for us to do."

– Ephesians 2:10 (NIV)

God has already walked out the steps of your life. Your job is simply to stay in step with Him. Another way to say this is that He has laid out the tracks for your life. Your job is to do your best to stay on track. I was on a train once, going through mountain tunnels. One of the tunnels was so long that it was pitch black inside with no light whatsoever. I wondered, how in the world could the conductor drive a train in total darkness, not even being able to see the end of the tunnel? The Lord gently said to me, "He has to trust the tracks." You see, long before he drove into that tunnel, the tracks had already been laid down, and his destination was already set. He didn't have to worry at all. His only job was to stay on the tracks.

When you walk with God, He makes every one of your steps firm. He keeps you from misstepping and from missing a step! And even when we disobey and stumble, because we are on a walk with Him, He reaches out and grabs us so that we won't fall. He keeps us on the tracks. God comforts us in the book of Isaiah by letting us know that He knows the end from the beginning and that His purpose for us will stand. God starts at the end of your life and works His way back to the beginning. In Ephesians, Paul reasserts this point. We are chosen and predestined according to plan. God will work out everything in our lives in conformity to His will. He has prepared, in advance, our purpose and our good works.

Live today in the confidence that the moment you accepted Jesus Christ as your Lord and Savior, it set off a covenant relationship with God that gave Him permission to lay out the tracks of your life. He vetoed some of your decisions because He knew you ultimately would desire His sovereign will above your own free will. He detoured you from certain relationships that would change the plan and purpose He has for your life. And He allowed some things you may never understand, but you will learn to accept, because you trust Him so deeply and completely. You will reach your destination in Him. Everything will work out in your favor. You will leave this world headed for a better world. And, you will have victory here before you go there. God has already written the end of your story. You win.

38 DAILY

"Then the Lord said to Moses, "I will rain down bread from heaven for you. The people are to go out each day and gather enough for that day. In this way, I will test them and see whether they will follow My instructions."

– Exodus 16:4 (NIV)

Walking with God means moving in obedience with His instructions daily. It's really quite simple, but harder to do than it sounds. Sometimes, even when God's instructions aren't complicated, our humanness becomes the biggest challenge. This scripture is a great example of a simple instruction made complicated by human weaknesses and thereby interrupting our walk with God.

The children of Israel were in the wilderness and food became an issue. God used this issue to test them to see if they would follow His instructions. Once they learned to obey God, they would be ready for their Promised Land. So, He provided bread from heaven for them with simple instructions. Gather enough for only one day, every day except Friday. On Friday they were to gather enough for Friday and Saturday which was their Sabbath Day when they were not to work. Then they were to start over on Sunday. The instruction was to do this daily. Of course, some tried to collect for extra days, and some went out on Saturday. Our humanness, our rebellion, our laziness, our greed, our inability to follow instructions makes our walk with God more complicated than it has to be.

Pray daily. Read the word, daily. Do right by people, daily. Show love, daily. It's really very simple. But we get bored, and distracted, and greedy, and rebellious, and doubtful, and tired, and a list of other things that make such simple instructions so complicated that we do not walk in humble obedience to God. If your desire is to walk with God and have this Enoch experience, then you must master the discipline of moving in obedience to His instructions daily. Start with just one instruction today. I would suggest prayer, but reading a scripture, or doing a good deed, or anything you know God would like, is fine. Let's continue to grow in our walk with God by doing just one thing right, at least today!

Naida M. Parson, Ph.D

39 ACCURATE OBEDIENCE

"But Samuel replied: "Does the Lord delight in burnt offerings and sacrifices as much as in obeying the Lord? To obey is better than sacrifice, and to heed is better than the fat of rams."

— 1 Samuel 15:22 (NIV)

Walking with God is as much about obeying His instructions as it is talking and communing with Him. Your goal is to always stay in step with Him. Even when you are doing other things that you think may please Him, you are out of step. Walking with God is more than the good or great things you do. It's the accuracy of what you do. It may be a good thing, but is it exactly what He said?

King Saul learned this the hard way. He went on a mission from God with some specific instructions. He did most of what God said, but he adjusted some of it for what sounded like a good reason to him. God told him to go against this nation and execute God's judgement against them. He was told to kill everything. But the soldiers talked him into saving some of the livestock so they could offer up sacrifices to God (amongst other things I'm sure). Partial obedience is disobedience. End of story. When Samuel came, he gave the king this powerful verse that has become a Christian staple. "To obey is better than sacrifice."

Today, go back over some things God has instructed you to do. It may be as simple as your prayer time, or reading a book, or treating someone better than you have before. It may be as complicated as instructions to start a ministry, or how to raise your children, or how to get healthy again. Whatever it is, be reminded that partial obedience is disobedience and do your best to line up with God's will for your life. And remember, there is so much grace in this walk with God. Don't beat yourself up for faltering, but don't make faltering a way of life, either. Accept God's grace and then make it your priority to walk with God in humble and accurate obedience. Practice doing right until you get it right.

40 EVEN THE SMALL THINGS

"The king assigned them a daily amount of food and wine from the king's table. They were to be trained for three years, and after that they were to enter the king's service.

But Daniel resolved not to defile himself with the royal food and wine, and he asked the chief official for permission not to defile himself this way."

– Daniel 1:5, 8 (NIV)

Walking with God is the daily challenge of staying in step with Him in everything you do. Even the small things like how you dress, places you go, and the food you eat. If you were in a royal family, you would understand fully that you don't have the freedom to conduct your life like "normal" or "common" people. You dress, act, talk and eat in a way that honors your royalty. Well, you are part of a royal family! You are required to behave in a way that honors God in everything you do. When you walk with God, your every step is to be within His will for you.

Daniel and the other Hebrew young men were captured and brought into slavery. The king of that country took the best of the best and wanted to assimilate them into Babylonian culture. But they remained strong in their walk with God and refused to get out of step with Him, even in a foreign land where they were slaves. They asked if they could not eat what the king had prepared and then challenged their captors by saying that they would look better than everyone else who was eating what the king provided.

Daniel resolved not to defile himself. I suppose that meant even if it cost him his life. What a challenge to remain faithful to God when your life is on the line, and you are under tremendous pressure to conform. There are many things that challenge us as human beings to go against God's will and get out of step. Today, think of another thing in your life that is not what God wants for you. Then resolve to follow God, no matter what. As we go through these devotions, my hope is that you will continue to make changes in your life until you are complete in your walk with God. Time to take another step, today.

Naida M. Parson, Ph.D

41 DON'T PULL AWAY

"I am the Vine; you are the branches. If you remain in Me and I in you, you will bear much fruit; apart from Me you can do nothing."

– John 15:5 (NIV)

Remaining, or abiding, in Jesus Christ is another way to talk about walking with God. The only way to truly have a relationship, that habitual fellowship with God which is what this devotional is about, is to do it through Jesus Christ. This is what makes us Christians. We believe that the ONLY way to God is through Jesus. As we approach God for relationship with Him, He sees us through His Son. His perfect, sinless Son. So, remaining in Jesus is our ultimate goal in life. When we accept Jesus, we instantly become everything God ever wanted us to be. How could that be? Because Jesus is everything God wanted all of us to be and we stand in Him.

So how do we remain in Jesus? He gives us the analogy of a grape vine with branches. As long as the branches are connected to the vine, everything in the vine flows into the branches and the branches produce fruit. Staying in the vine means not pulling away and separating. Wherever the vine is, the branches follow. When you do your own thing instead of obeying God's instruction through His word, and through the leading of the Holy Spirit living in you, you separate, or pull away from, the Vine. When you drift into distraction and stop praying, and communicating, and spending time with God, you pull away from the Vine. When you place anything, or anybody, above God in your priorities, in your worship, or in your preference, you pull away from the Vine.

Remain in Him. Abide in Him. Stay in contact. Listen for His voice and determine never to drift away. Our self-centered desires pull us away. Our schedules, our families, our responsibilities, and our own internal struggles can pull us away from God. You may be involved in some sin that has taken your attention. Or you may be involved in doing lots of good things that have distracted you from making Him priority. Don't pull away. Don't allow yourself to be pulled away. Rededicate yourself today to simply abiding with Jesus. You know by now what that means. Spend time with Him today and turn your heart back towards the only thing that matters in the long run. Walking with God through Jesus Christ.

42 GIVE YOUR SPIRIT A FIGHTING CHANCE

"So, I say, walk by the Spirit, and you will not gratify the desires of the flesh. For the flesh desires what is contrary to the Spirit, and the Spirit what is contrary to the flesh. They are in conflict with each other, so that you are not to do whatever you want."

– Galatians 5:16-17 (NIV)

I'm sure by now you have grown in your walk with God. I'm sure you have begun to have an Enoch experience. But I am just as sure that some days you have missed the mark. I'm sure that you still spend lots of time out of step. If not, great! You're ahead of the game. But if you find yourself struggling with your walk at times, I need you to know why. You have to expect your flesh to fight this.

Let me explain. When you were born again, you were born of the Spirit and the Holy Spirit came to reside in your human spirit causing it to be renewed and made alive to God. That gave you a new spiritual nature. But the old you (the old nature) still exists. We are to treat it like its dead, according to scripture. We are to stop feeding it and letting it rule us. We are to symbolically crucify it, mortify it, and deny it. But crucifixion can be a slow process. In the meantime, the flesh (the old sinful nature) and the born-again spirit will fight with each other daily to win over your will. When we are strong in our spirit, it wins, and we make right decisions. When we are weak in the spirit, the flesh might win, and we make wrong decisions.

That's why I want to keep reminding you that there is so much grace in this walk. If you stumble or falter, just get back in the fight. Do the things that build up your spirit and starve your flesh. The more you starve your flesh, the weaker it gets. Then you walk more and more in the Holy Spirit, and you will not keep gratifying the flesh. Many people give up the fight and just do whatever they want. But the Bible says that kind of thinking leads to spiritual death. You want to walk with God because you love Him, and you are in relationship with Him. You don't want to live any more in your flesh. There is no fruit there and no future, either. So today, your challenge is to choose one thing that you know your flesh feeds on and erase it from your life. A show, or a habit, or a relationship, or an activity. Surrender it to God and give your spirit a fighting chance.

Naida M. Parson, Ph.D

43   FIGHT BACK

"For our struggle is not against flesh and blood, but against the rulers, against the authorities, against the powers of this dark world and against the spiritual forces of evil in the heavenly realms."

– Ephesians 6:12 (NIV)

Our own old nature, our flesh, is not the only thing that fights against our walk with God. Many people think it's fanatical and too literal to believe in the existence of demons. A horror movie once stated that the most effective trick Satan had ever used was to convince people he did not exist. I know demonic forces exist. Jesus said they did. The Bible says they do. One of the major signs that follow believers is our ability to cast out demons. There are demons who are assigned to oppose your walk with God.

The writer of Ephesians wanted us to know this. He wanted us to know that our fight is not against flesh and blood. This time the word flesh does not refer to our old sinful nature. In this context, the world flesh paired with blood means that we do not fight against human beings in this spiritual struggle. We are fighting against demonic evil powers in the spirit realm. These demons speak to us, tempt us, distract us, and deceive us. We are to be aware of them and protect ourselves against them.

Expect to have to do spiritual warfare to maintain your walk with God. We have the power to rebuke demons. We have the power to bind them, which means to render them inoperative. We can take authority over them and resist them. They have been defeated at the cross! So, notice today when your thoughts are drawing you away from your walk and know that they may not be your thoughts at all. Notice when you just don't want to pray, or read scripture, or worship for any particular reason and know that might be an evil influence outside of you. Notice when you are distracted, or disturbed, or unexpectedly interrupted and know that there may be a calculated plan that you have the power to cancel in the Name of Jesus. Remember that the last thing the devil wants is for you to walk with God. But also, be confident that he cannot stop you as long as you fight back.

44 MINDSET

"Those who live according to the flesh have their minds set on what the flesh desires; but those who live in accordance with the Spirit have their minds set on what the Spirit desires. The mind governed by the flesh is death, but the mind governed by the Spirit is life and peace. The mind governed by the flesh is hostile to God; it does not submit to God's law, nor can it do so."

— Romans 8:5-7 (NIV)

What is your mindset? How do you think and what has that caused you to routinely do? Your flesh and the demons that fight against your spiritual walk both work together to keep your mind set on earthly, non-spiritual things. They have you in a certain routine. The things you eat and drink, the places you go, and the way you spend your time can become very routine. We all have our morning rituals and the way we wind down at night. So, fitting into your life a walk with God can sometimes be difficult if it doesn't fit into your routine.

Paul calls this a mindset. You have your mind set on the things your old nature desires. You build your life around those desires. But now that you are dedicating your life to the things of the Holy Spirit, you must change your focus and many of your routines. Now you go after the things of the Spirit. You think about spiritual things and engage more in spiritual activities. You have more spiritual priorities, and the direction of your life moves away from your desires to God's desires.

Look at your life today. Look at your routines and priorities. Look at your desires. Write down 5 of your biggest goals in life and the things you are doing now toward those goals. Now compare them to what Jesus would want for your life. Better yet, pray today about the things Jesus wants for your life and begin to align your routines and priorities to be more of what He wants you to be. Those things are already in your spirit. Get your mind set on those things. It will help you submit more to God, and it will lead to life and peace.

Naida M. Parson, Ph.D

45 A CHANGE IN ROUTINE

"So, Elisha left him and went back. He took his yoke of oxen and slaughtered them. He burned the plowing equipment to cook the meat and gave it to the people, and they ate. Then he set out to follow Elijah and became his servant."

– 1 Kings 19:21 (NIV)

"When Simon Peter saw this, he fell at Jesus' knees and said, "Go away from me, Lord; I am a sinful man!" For he and all his companions were astonished at the catch of fish they had taken, and so were James and John, the sons of Zebedee, Simon's partners. Then Jesus said to Simon, "Don't be afraid; from now on you will fish for people." So, they pulled their boats up on shore, left everything, and followed Him."

– Luke 5:8-11 (NIV)

They say that interruption is the privilege of authority. When you have authority, you have the right to intrude on, and interrupt, anything under your authority. I had a tight schedule one night and my plane was landing right on time. But then, it had to circle for a while because the President of the United States was taking off in Air Force One! It didn't matter that it got the rest of us behind schedule. Interruption is the privilege of authority. When we were young and our parents walked in the room with some instructions, it didn't matter that we were in the middle of our television program and were going to miss the best part. Everything stopped and we complied because interruption is the privilege of authority.

Elisha knew this. Peter, Andrew, James, and John knew this. For Elisha the call on his life was about to begin. He met the prophet Elijah and knew that he was called to be the next prophet. He was working at the time driving oxen and was interrupted. He killed the oxen and burned the yoke and left everything and followed Elijah. The first disciples were at work as well. It was their routine. But they met Jesus and were called to catch men instead of fish. They left their nets, and everything else, and followed Jesus for the next three years. For the rest of their lives, they were in service to Him.

Following Jesus will change your routine. He has the right because He has the authority. He will interrupt your life! He is going to require a prayer time and some major life changes. He may interrupt the way you live, from who you associate with, to the words you use, to how you eat and drink. He may change your profession, where you live, or even your chosen denomination. He most certainly will interrupt your day with instructions, moments alone with Him, prayers, praise, or opportunities to witness or encourage someone. Walking with God will change your routine, so today, be open to every nudge from the Spirit that God wants a moment of your day. Open your schedule to Him today in prayer and see what He places there. Then make His request your new routine.

46 A CHANGE IN PLANS

"In the sixth month of Elizabeth's pregnancy, God sent the angel Gabriel to Nazareth, a town in Galilee, to a virgin pledged to be married to a man named Joseph, a descendant of David. The virgin's name was Mary. The angel went to her and said, "Greetings, you who are highly favored! The Lord is with you."

You will conceive and give birth to a Son, and you are to call Him Jesus.

"I am the Lord's servant," Mary answered. "May your word to me be fulfilled." Then the angel left her."

— Luke 1:26-28, 31, 38 (NIV)

Your walk with God is going to require that you be flexible. He typically doesn't let you know all the plans He has for you, and all the directions for your life, all at once. He wants us to walk with Him daily and depend on His guidance. Of course, there are things He will reveal to us to plan for and execute, but there are also some things He has in store for you that you may never imagine. You will have to be willing, not only to change your routine, but to change a lifelong plan. Or perhaps, to change the plan for a season in your life.

Mary, the mother of Jesus, certainly had some plans. She was a young girl waiting on her dream of marriage and family like every Jewish young woman, I suppose. She was to marry a local carpenter. He was a just and principled man. Perhaps she knew her father had chosen well for her, and she was looking forward to a predictable life. And then God interrupted. She had been chosen for a purpose greater than she could have imagined. She was to bring the Messiah into the world. She would be pregnant by the Holy Spirit. It was a pretty far-fetched story, but after a few questions she said, "may your word to me be fulfilled." She changed the whole focus of her life because she walked in obedience to God.

If you are determined to walk with God, you must be flexible. This may be as simple as changing your breakfast plans, or where you go after work today. It may be as drastic as moving to another city or spending your life on a mission field. It could be marriage when you don't feel ready, or prolonged singleness when that's not how you saw your life panning out. Listen to God today and be ready and willing for whatever He may lead you to do. Be flexible. That doesn't mean you don't plan. It means you submit your plans to Him and always include Him before you plan at all. I guarantee you that wherever He leads there are great blessings to follow.

47 BE FLEXIBLE

"Whether you turn to the right or to the left, your ears will hear a Voice behind you, saying, "This is the way; walk in it.""

– Isaiah 30:21 (NIV)

In order to walk with God, you must be flexible. You may be led to do things you have never done before. Or perhaps to do the same things, but in different ways. Maybe you always stayed up late at night and slept late in the morning, but God decides to turn you into a morning person because that's a better and more focused time where He can commune with you. Or you may be a person who rises early, but so does everyone else in your house, so He doesn't get quality time until the house is asleep at night and that's when He wants your attention. Maybe you're a friendly person who is always surrounded by people and God may call you to be more isolative for periods of time. Or, you could be the loner type, but God instructs you to get out among the people.

This scripture in Isaiah talks about a time when Israel will again walk with God. They will hear from God again telling them which direction to go. To the left or to the right will depend on what they hear from their Master and King. God has a way of speaking plainly to us as we walk with Him. So many moments in our lives we will hear Him say "this is the way". He speaks in many ways, but you will know. If we are going to go where He goes, we must have an ear to hear Him and be willing to switch directions at His command.

Today, determine that your walk with God will be the most important thing in your life. Decide once, and for all, that you will say yes to His direction no matter what. It will require you to be flexible. You will have to be willing to change directions at a moment's notice. That may be as simple as driving to work, or home, a different way. It may be stopping to share with someone when you didn't think you had the time. It may be something bigger like changing jobs or moving to a new city. But it doesn't matter where God's will takes you as long as He is there. In your prayer today, ask Him to show you the right way for you and then walk in it. It is the most important thing you will ever pursue.

48 STAY IN PURSUIT

"Then Moses said, "Now show me Your glory.""

– Exodus 33:18 (NIV)

Are you in pursuit of God? Do you want to know Him better? Are you fascinated with Him? Moses was. He had been through some things already. The burning bush. The plagues. The exodus from Egypt. The Red Sea. Manna and water and quail. But there was so much more to know about God. Moses wanted to know His ways. He wanted to live in the favor of God even deeper than he already did. He wanted to see God's glory. Why? It appears that maybe it was just for the purpose of relationship.

God invites us to pursue Him. Often, He asks us to come. In Isaiah, He said that all who were thirsty should come. Jesus said all who were weary and burdened could come and find rest. Even in the last book of the Bible He says He stands at the door and knocks and if we would just open the door, He would come in. We can know God as well as we would like to. Many people knew Jesus, but the twelve were closer. Of the twelve, three drew even closer. Of the three, one drew closest to Him out of them all. Martha was close to Jesus. He spent time at her house. But Mary drew closer. She spent time at His feet.

Pursue intimacy with your God today. Ask Him to show Himself to you in ways that you haven't known Him before. Study the word in a deeper way, looking for things about Him you've never noticed before. Pray in a way that isn't about what you need from Him but is more about what you want to know about Him. Ask Him to teach you His ways and to show you His glory. Jesus is Lord and Savior, but He is also a very good Friend. The way you work on a friendship is to spend time, ask questions, listen for the answer, and stay in pursuit.

Naida M. Parson, Ph.D

49 BE WILLING TO CHANGE YOUR LIFE

"But Noah found favor in the eyes of the Lord.

So, God said to Noah, "I am going to put an end to all people, for the earth is filled with violence because of them. I am surely going to destroy both them and the earth. So, make yourself an ark of cypress wood; make rooms in it and coat it with pitch inside and out. This is how you are to build it: The ark is to be three hundred cubits long, fifty cubits wide and thirty cubits high.

Noah did everything just as God commanded him."

— Genesis 6:8, 13-15, 22 (NIV)

Walking with God is a journey. There are many stops and starts along the way. There will be changes in direction. There may even be a revelation of a season, or a purpose, in your life that might catch you by surprise. If you are willing to continue your walk with God, then get ready to experience a change in your routine. He may surprise you from time to time. He knows what your destiny is, but He may reveal it to you only a small bit at a time. Then there is that day that a big switch may come that breaks up your everyday life.

I don't know what Noah's daily routine was prior to this day when God decided to let him know he had found favor. He was the head of the only family that would survive a massive judgment by God. God was going to wipe out every other human life on the earth and start over. Whatever Noah's routine was, I do know that God was about to drastically change it. Now Noah was called upon to build a large boat called an ark. God gave him exactly how it was to be built, what it was to be made of, and what to do to collect the living things God was starting over with. In one conversation with God, Noah's daily activities were completely changed.

Walking with God is an exciting journey, but most things that are exciting can also be very scary. If you can trust Him with your life … if you can trust Him with your destiny … walk closely with Him, even if the turns are sharp and the change is huge. I promise you that you will find purpose. You will become the best you. You will find that the favor of God will take you places you never dreamed of, have you do things you never imagined, and reveal to you things about you that you would have never known. How could Noah have imagined that just by walking with God every human being on earth would be biologically connected to him? How will you ever know your hidden greatness unless you walk with the One who makes you great? Listen today for His instruction and be willing to change your life.

50 A TOTALLY DIFFERENT DIRECTION

"Then Ananias went to the house and entered it. Placing his hands on Saul, he said, "Brother Saul, the Lord—Jesus, who appeared to you on the road as you were coming here—has sent me so that you may see again and be filled with the Holy Spirit." Immediately, something like scales fell from Saul's eyes, and he could see again. He got up and was baptized,

At once he began to preach in the synagogues that Jesus is the Son of God."

— Acts 9:17-18, 20 (NIV)

They say that having a baby changes everything. Nothing in your life will ever be the same once you become a parent. It not only changes your sleeping habits, your leisure time, your financial status, and the shows you watch on television, but it also changes your heart, your focus, your priorities, and the things you worry about. And it doesn't last just for the 18 years or so they are your responsibility. The older they get, the more complicated their issues get and sometimes the more your heart aches for them and the decisions they make. The joys are tremendous and so are the let downs. You never know which one you're going to get. But you do know that the minute you found out this baby was coming, everything changed.

Having a walk with God changes everything. The minute you accept the Lord Jesus, your focus, your priorities, and yes perhaps even your sleeping habits and what you watch on television, all experience a drastic change. Like brother Saul in our scripture. You may know him as the Apostle Paul. His walk with God even changed his name! His life was going in a totally different direction. He was against Christianity and even put people in jail and consented to their execution. But one day he met Jesus for himself. God arrested him while he was on his way to arrest others. He was convinced that Jesus was indeed the Messiah and that changed everything. Now he was the biggest fan and contributor to the very movement he opposed so violently. Walking with God changes everything.

Offer the direction of your life to God again today. Make a fresh commitment to follow Him. Let your walk with God change your priorities. Wake up earlier to talk and commune with Him. Submit your entertainment to Him down to what you watch on television. Give Him access to your music, your thought life, your relationships, the way you spend your money, and your major concerns in life. Let Him change the way you do marriage, and parenting, and work. If you have not changed at all, you are not walking with Him. You may have missed a turn or two. But that's okay because He knows where you are and if you recommit today, He will help you get in step with Him.

51 | FOLLOW INSTRUCTIONS

"One day Ruth's mother-in-law Naomi said to her, "My daughter, I must find a home for you, where you will be well provided for. Now Boaz, with whose women you have worked, is a relative of ours. Tonight, he will be winnowing barley on the threshing floor. Wash, put on perfume, and get dressed in your best clothes. Then go down to the threshing floor, but don't let him know you are there until he has finished eating and drinking. When he lies down, note the place where he is lying. Then go and uncover his feet and lie down. He will tell you what to do." "I will do whatever you say," Ruth answered. So, she went down to the threshing floor and did everything her mother-in-law told her to do."

– Ruth 3:1-6 (NIV)

As you walk with God, He will give you instructions for everything He has preordained for you to do and to be. You must realize that every instruction is important and has its rewards. He may speak to you from the Bible, His written word, or from strong impressions in your spirit, or even in an audible voice. But God also speaks to you through His people. You may get very specific instructions by way of the wisdom of a mentor, pastor, prophet, or perhaps an older much wiser person whom God makes sure crosses your path with just the right answer. However He speaks, deep inside, you will know it comes from Him.

This was the case with Ruth. After the death of her husband, she followed her mother-in-law, Naomi, back to live amongst God's people, Israel. She accepted Jehovah as her God and decided to walk with Him. At this point, it was time for her to step again into the role of a wife. Who would have known she was stepping into being a direct ancestor to Jesus Christ? So, Naomi gives her step-by-step instruction on how to get a wealthy man to marry her and keep her in the family. She followed the instructions and soon was a married woman with child.

The most essential step to success is simply to ask God what to do and do exactly what He says. Every instruction has a purpose and a reward attached to it. God is very intentional, and His plans have so many moving parts we can never fully understand why He says what He says and does what He does until we look back and see the full picture. Our part is to trust Him.

Our part is to obey. Our part is to walk step by step with Him. Our part is to abide in Him. He controls and orchestrates the rest. Today, look back over some of God's past instructions to you and see where you need to get in step. Make that commitment today. There is a reason and a reward.

Naida M. Parson, Ph.D

52 IT'S NOT ALWAYS AN EASY WIN

"Moses returned to the Lord and said, "Why, Lord, why have You brought trouble on this people? Is this why You sent me? Ever since I went to Pharaoh to speak in Your Name, he has brought trouble on this people, and You have not rescued Your people at all.""

— Exodus 5:22-23 (NIV)

"Then the Lord said to Moses, "Now you will see what I will do to Pharaoh: Because of My mighty hand he will let them go; because of My mighty hand he will drive them out of his country.""

— Exodus 6:1 (NIV)

Sometimes when walking with God, you will be sure of His direction, and everything will work out miraculously well. And sometimes, things will get even more difficult for a season. We think because it doesn't come easy, God didn't say it. We expect every instruction of God to come with immediate victory and easy wins. But there are some things in God's will that we have to fight for. Sometimes, we have to hold on until the timing is right.

Moses was asked by God to go to the king of Egypt, called the Pharaoh, and demand that he let the Hebrew slaves go so they could worship their own God. It was clearly God's instruction. It was clearly God's will. But, when Moses went and did what God said, the Pharaoh didn't let them go. In fact, everything got worse. The Egyptians treated them harshly and the work got harder. The people Moses was sent to help were furious and everything seemed to have gone left! But that's not how the story ended. God did eventually come through on His promise and they all went free with plenty of wealth as compensation for years of hard labor.

Just because things are not smooth and easy doesn't mean that God did not give the instruction. Sometimes, He is creating patience and strength in us. Sometimes, we have to get the ball rolling and then wait for the right timing. Sometimes, it's a fight and not an easy win. Sometimes, it's the fight that makes us ready to handle the promise when it finally comes. So today, determine to stick with God's instruction and don't doubt Him if it becomes difficult. Fight through it. Hang on to it. Be diligent to do exactly what He says. It will work out and the promised reward will come. Keep walking with Him and you will get there.

53   THE MANUFACTURER'S MANUAL

"If you fully obey the Lord your God and carefully follow all His commands I give you today, the Lord your God will set you high above all the nations on earth. All these blessings will come on you and accompany you if you obey the Lord your God: You will be blessed in the city and blessed in the country.

You will be blessed when you come in and blessed when you go out."

— Deuteronomy 28:1-3, 6 (NIV)

There is tremendous blessing in walking with God. His part is to bless you in every area of your life. Your part is to be diligent to do what He says. God knows how He created us, and His laws and commands are like the owner's manual to an appliance. Only the manufacturer can tell you how to use their product to its best capability because the manufacturer knows its design. There are some things that the manual will tell you not to do. The instructions may seem restrictive, but they are necessary for the appliance to work like it was intended. All of God's laws and commands are for our benefit. They are from our Creator and are consistent with our design. The world we live in sees many of these laws as restrictive, but we understand that they insure we can live our best lives.

When the Nation of Israel was preparing to go into their Promised Land, Moses wanted to give them one more pep talk before leaving the scene. He urged them to obey God's commandments and shared with them the rewards if they did. Of course, we know that they couldn't, and they didn't. But, had they given it their best try, God's grace would have covered the rest for them. All God really wanted was their hearts. He would have helped them with the rest. All God really wants from you is your heart as well, and if you falter, His grace will help you with the rest.

So, give God your best effort to follow His instructions, today. He knows you may falter at times but be diligent to get it right as much as lies in you. There will be great blessing for your life in the long run. He knows what will truly make you happy. He knows what will give you peace and joy. His instructions may seem restrictive, but the special way you are designed requires some restrictions, just like the things that man manufactures. That's the whole point of having the manual. So today be diligent. Be very careful to follow His commands. Your blessings will overtake you.

Naida M. Parson, Ph.D

54 | WHAT IF I MISS GOD?

"I press on toward the goal to win the prize for which God has called me heavenward in Christ Jesus. All of us, then, who are mature should take such a view of things. And if on some point you think differently, that too God will make clear to you. Only let us live up to what we have already attained."

– Philippians 3:14-16 (NIV)

Walking faithfully with God means following His lead and instructions. It means obeying whatever He has said as it is revealed to you through His Word, through the inner guidance of the Holy Spirit, or through an answer to prayer that may come by way of another believer, pastor, prophet, or teacher. But what if you miss God? What if the answer or directive you have did not come from Him? The best of us have believed God was speaking when in fact He wasn't. Even in reading His written words, there are times when we finally get a true revelation on a scripture we had previously taken a different way. For the fearful, this can be a paralyzing dilemma.

In Paul's letter to the Philippians, he tells of his determination to know Christ to the point that he counts everything else as garbage. He just wants to press toward the mark of his high calling and forget everything that was behind him. He says that all of us who are mature should be like minded. He then makes a statement that should bring us all comfort. It is a principle we can live by. He says that if anyone is of another mindset, God will make that clear to you. Another translation says that if you are ever "otherwise minded" God will reveal that to you also. If we are serious about walking with God, He will make sure we don't miss Him. He will correct us. He will turn us in the right direction. His will doesn't have to be a guessing game.

When you have an instruction from God, just do it by faith if you believe that's what He said and trust Him to show you if you missed Him. He is faithful. He is for you. He wants you to succeed more than you want to yourself. He wants you to walk with Him more than you want Him to walk with you. So, trust that if you are ever "otherwise minded," or if you ever think differently than God about any issue or decision, He will make it clear to you. God can speak plainly. So go ahead and do what you already know to do. Live up to what you have already attained and push forward for more. Trust that God will not let you get off track as long as your heart is to walk with Him.

55 TEACH ME YOUR WAYS

"If You are pleased with me, teach me Your ways so I may know You and continue to find favor with You ...

– Exodus 33:13 (NIV)

Sometimes knowing what God wants from our lives is a difficult task. As we walk with Him, there comes a time when we must make life changing decisions. We know we must acknowledge Him, and He will direct us, but when we want something so bad it may be hard to determine if it's us, or if it's God. We can then get fearful and began to wonder if we're going to really mess this thing up. Let this comfort you, as long as your motives are right, He won't let you make a wrong destiny move, or a devastating mistake.

Moses was at a crossroads in his leadership journey. God was frustrated with His people and was testing Moses saying that He would not go with them into the Promised Land. But He still wanted Moses to lead them. Moses didn't want to make a wrong move, and perhaps, Moses also was confused about what God really wanted from him in this season in his life. So, he did what we all can do in our walk with God. He asked Him to show him His ways and how to continue in His favor. Moses was saying, "teach me Your ways because I don't like being in this place of not knowing what You want or how to stay in Your favor."

Let that be your prayer today. "Lord, teach me Your ways." We want God to teach us His way of doing things and His way of thinking about things and people. Teach us, Lord, how to love like You love and feel what You feel. As we work, and play, and interact with people, show us, teach us, and change us so that we can stay in Your favor. That's where we want to be. We trust God to not allow us to make any mistakes that will devastate our future and change the direction of our lives away from His will. And He will answer that prayer because He is pleased with us, simply because we have chosen to walk with Him.

Naida M. Parson, Ph.D

56 KNOWING GOD'S HEART

"Now this is eternal life: that they know You, the only true God, and Jesus Christ, whom You have sent."

– John 17:3 (NIV)

There is so much more to God than church, and ministry, and theology. God wants you to know Him. God wants you to be intimate with Him. God wants you to know what makes Him happy, what causes Him frustration, and what breaks His heart. In my walk with God, I have learned some intimate things about Him because I ask Him intimate questions and He reveals to me His heart.

For example, one thing that breaks the heart of God is anytime someone dies without knowing Him. It is not His will that any should perish. He wants all of mankind to come to a place of repentance (a change of heart, mind, and direction away from sin and towards Him). Death is separation from God. Christians don't die because they are never separated from Him. Sinners are separated already. So, when they die, any chance they have of knowing Him as a loving Father is lost forever.

God is relational. He loves His children… all of them. Even those who do not want Him because they have been blinded by the devil or their own wicked desires. Every time one of His wayward children passes into eternity, the heart of God is broken. Knowing His heart should shape our days and fill us with the desire to reach one more with the good news. The good news is that we have a Father waiting for us so He can love us eternally. What can we do to ease the heart of God? Today, walk closer to God by asking Him to connect you with someone who does not know Him. We can ease the heart of the God we love by introducing someone new to Him. Let your relationship with God begin to shape your life's mission.

57 THERE IS GRACE IN THIS WALK

"Then the Lord spoke to Job out of the storm. He said: "Who is this that obscures My plans with words without knowledge? Brace yourself like a man; I will question you, and you shall answer Me. "Where were you when I laid the earth's foundation? Tell Me if you understand."

– Job 38:1-4 (NIV)

"My ears had heard of You but now my eyes have seen You. Therefore, I despise myself and repent in dust and ashes."

"After the Lord had said these things to Job, he said to Eliphaz the Temanite, "I am angry with you and your two friends, because you have not spoken the truth about Me, as My servant Job has. So now take seven bulls and seven rams and go to My servant Job and sacrifice a burnt offering for yourselves. My servant Job will pray for you, and I will accept his prayer and not deal with you according to your folly. You have not spoken the truth about Me, as my servant Job has."

"After Job had prayed for his friends, the LORD restored his fortunes and gave him twice as much as he had before."

"The Lord blessed the latter part of Job's life more than the former part. He had fourteen thousand sheep, six thousand camels, a thousand yoke of oxen and a thousand donkeys. And he also had seven sons and three daughters."

– Job 42:5-6, 10, 12-13 (NIV)

When walking with God and attempting to stay in step with Him daily you are bound to mess up. You may skip several days of prayer. You may have seasons of disobedience. You may get angry with God and lose faith. You won't feel like talking to Him some days, and other days it will feel like He doesn't want to talk to you. You will fail Him. You will. But don't let your human frailty discourage you from your walk. It is difficult and He knows that, but there is so much grace in

Naida M. Parson, Ph.D

it. Grace is when God gives you something you don't deserve, like forgiving you and staying in relationship with you, even when you really mess up.

Job was said to be a perfect and upright man. However, in watching how he went through his testing, it doesn't seem that way. He complained. He wished for death. He accused God. He questioned God. He pouted. He was downright pitiful, and understandably so. He really had not done anything wrong to cause God to test him so severely. He started out the perfect servant. He declared, that just like he accepted good from God, he would accept the evil. The Lord gave and the Lord had the right to take away. Naked he came into the world and naked he would return. But, after things went from bad to worse, Job had some moments that didn't resemble a perfect loving walk with God.

However, God's grace and mercy didn't hold it against him. God knew He had allowed the unthinkable into Job's life. Job passed the test because he never cursed God and he never stopped believing. He stayed in relationship, even though he accused God of being unfair. He spoke the truth about God because he knew Him. They had relationship. He did have some harsh words for God, but after God corrected him, Job knew he had gone too far. He apologized and repented and stood corrected. And God forgave him, restored him, defended him in front of his accusers, favored his prayers, and blessed him double in the end. So, today, no matter what has happened, or how you may have messed up, keep walking with God. There is so much grace in this walk! Thank You, Lord! No matter how long it's been since you've prayed, God is waiting for your return. No matter what misbehaving you have done, come right back into fellowship. Apologize. Repent. Grace is waiting for you.

58 JUST CONTINUE TO WALK

"Because of the LORD's great love, we are not consumed, for His compassions never fail. They are new every morning; great is Your faithfulness. I say to myself, "The LORD is my portion; therefore, I will wait for Him." The LORD is good to those whose hope is in Him, to the one who seeks Him; it is good to wait quietly for the salvation of the LORD."

– Lamentations 3:22-26 (NIV)

Never let anything come between you and your daily walk with God. No matter how bad a day your yesterday was. No matter what sin you may have committed, or how you have failed. Start over every day without guilt, or shame, or disappointment. God is always eager to be with you. He may correct you, but He won't reject you. Every sin you have committed has already been forgiven. There is no shame because His blood has erased the transgression. And there is no disappointment because there isn't anything you have done that caught Him by surprise.

If anyone could have disappointed Him, it would have been His chosen people, Israel. Oh, how He lavished them with love, and favor, and miracles, and blessings. He gave them choice land even at the expense of others. But they turned their backs on Him and worshiped idol gods. They followed people who didn't know the True and Living God, and they lived immorally and dishonestly. Still, as Jeremiah speaks out of his sadness for Israel, he declares the mercy of God. He recalls something about God that gives Him hope. His compassions don't fail. They are new every morning. This means God is so merciful and compassionate toward us that He doesn't hold a grudge even overnight. Every day can be a new day and a new walk with Him.

Wait for Him. Hope in Him. Seek Him. Everyday continue your walk with God no matter what. If you messed up tell Him about it and don't pretend you can hide it from Him. Be open to what He has to say. Look for what He will show you. You might be surprised at how compassionate and patient He is. Just like a parent potty training a toddler, they expect some mishaps, messes, and even some unnecessary defiance. But, every morning, they are at it again with no love lost, no relationship diminished, and no grudge, or bitterness, or scolding. They just keep loving, and training, and hoping that today will be better. So run to your Father today without guilt, shame, or fear. And no matter how today turns out, show up again tomorrow.

Naida M. Parson, Ph.D

59 DON'T LET GUILT HINDER YOUR WALK

"Then the man and his wife heard the sound of the LORD God as He was walking in the garden in the cool of the day, and they hid from the LORD God among the trees of the garden."

– Genesis 3:8 (NIV)

When Adam and Eve were created, they were in wonderful relationship with God. That was indeed the whole point of creating them. God is creative and relational. It stands to reason that He would create something He could relate to. It seems that they walked with God in the garden He had prepared for them because they knew the sound of His "walk". But this day was different. They had sinned. They disobeyed God. The consequence was a loss of innocence. They now knew something they had never known before: guilt and shame. So, they hid from God. They had always been naked, but now they are ashamed.

Guilt hinders your walk with God and takes away the joy of it. There should be unspeakable joy in your relationship with God, but when you have difficulty letting go of guilt, you will be more apt to hide from Him than run to Him. Hiding may take the form of going several days, or weeks, without praying. It may mean months, or years, of not going to church. It may mean delaying ministry because you feel unworthy or feeling that your behavior has lost you the favor of God.

But remember, you can't surprise God by your behavior. There was no gasp in heaven of shock or disbelief. When God called you to Him, He knew every mistake you would make, every sin you would ever commit, and every assignment you would mess up. He knew every fault and every failure. Yet, He called you. Yet, He saved you. And yet, He waits for you to get over the guilt and shame and come back and walk with Him. So today, and any day you feel guilty and ashamed, and think it best not to approach God, think again and come boldly to Him. Jesus has already made things right between you and God. All you have to do is come out from behind the trees and walk.

60 SO EXCITED TO BE WITH YOU

"A man was there by the name of Zacchaeus; he was a chief tax collector and was wealthy. He wanted to see who Jesus was, but because he was short, he could not see over the crowd. So, he ran ahead and climbed a sycamore-fig tree to see Him, since Jesus was coming that way. When Jesus reached the spot, He looked up and said to him, "Zacchaeus, come down immediately. I must stay at your house today."

Jesus said to him, "Today salvation has come to this house, because this man, too, is a son of Abraham. For the Son of Man came to seek and to save the lost.""

– Luke 19:2-5, 9-10 (NIV)

God is excited about every day He gets to spend time with you! He wants you to know Him. He enjoys your company. Even when we aren't mindful of Him, He comes looking for us. He crosses our mind, not because our minds are drawn to Him, but because He is drawn to us. He COMES across our minds. Our minds do not seek Him. It's His movement toward us that keeps us connected. We were created for this very purpose. We were created to walk with Him daily. You don't have to be afraid to approach Him no matter what your condition. Come to Him confident that every time, every day, every moment, He wants to be with you.

It's even better when the feeling is mutual, like it was with Zacchaeus. He wasn't a good person by human standards. He was a traitor to his nation. He stole from his own people as he collected taxes for the nation that had colonized them. But he was curious about Jesus. He wanted to see Him so much that he climbed a tree because he was too short to see Jesus over the large crowd. Little did he know that Jesus was just as excited about meeting him. Even though he was not a good person in his own eyes, Jesus was excited to spend time with him because there is something about spending time with Jesus that changes your life! Jesus found him in the tree and asked to go to his house that day.

Jesus will find you, too. Wherever you are, and whatever you have gotten yourself into, is of no consequence to God. He is excited that you have opened this book today, and that your heart wants to walk with Him. He wants to be with you. He wants to walk with you. He wants His relationship with you to be a transforming experience every day. So, take heart in the amazing fact that God is excited about your time together today. Let that fact make you run to Him in prayer right now. Do it now. He is waiting for you. And He is so excited!

Naida M. Parson, Ph.D

61 HE IS JUST THAT IN TO YOU

"Are not two sparrows sold for a penny? Yet not one of them will fall to the ground outside your Father's care. And even the very hairs of your head are all numbered. So don't be afraid; you are worth more than many sparrows."

– Matthew 10:29-31 (NIV)

Why would God want to spend time with you? Why does He pull you into relationship with Him? Why would He care whether you come to Him daily or not? He is great and awesome. He doesn't need anything you could possibly give Him. So, what is all of this about prayer and personal relationship? The answer is simple. He is just that in to you.

On the occasion of the scripture we read today, Jesus was trying to explain to His disciples their worth to God. He compares them to sparrows which were what we may call in our day "a dime a dozen." Pretty cheap and inconsequential. But of the sparrow, Jesus says not one of them fall without God being aware of it and caring about it. Then He says about us that God is so in to us, even the hairs on our head are numbered. He has numbered the hairs on your head! He is so into the details of your life that He knows when you've lost two hairs and how many you now have left!

God is so in to you that He gave you the best He had in His Son Jesus. He is so in to you that He chose you long before you had the slightest knowledge of Who He even was. He watches your every move, sees your thoughts before you think them, and weighs everything that happens to you before it can be allowed. He wants to be with you. He loves you. He is so in to you, and He simply asks that you walk with Him. It's the ultimate honor. It's the great unmerited favor. So, oblige Him and honor His request by spending even more time with Him today. Pick a special time and meet Him there. It's amazing to be so loved.

62 THE FORGIVING FORGETFULNESS OF GOD

"I, even I, am He who blots out your transgressions, for My own sake, and remembers your sins no more."

— Isaiah 43:25 (NIV)

Sometimes when you walk with God you will make missteps. Actually, that tends to happen when you have neglected your walk, but in our humanness, we are going to make mistakes. Sometimes we just make bad choices. Like Adam and Eve in the garden of Eden, our tendency will be to shy away from God and not meet with Him for a while. We are ashamed and disappointed in ourselves, and we are sure God is disappointed in us as well.

But I have found that He will take you for a walk even if you messed up the day before. Nothing catches Him by surprise anyway. It's not like you caught Him off guard. He doesn't add up your transgressions. For His own sake He doesn't let them pile up. When He blots out your transgressions, He erases them. In those days they wrote on parchment with ink. If you wanted to erase you would put a cloth in oil and blot the ink off the page. Then you could write over it like it was never there. I am so grateful for the forgiving forgetfulness of God. He makes the choice to forgive us, cleanse us, and count it as if it never happened.

God is only interested in one thing with you and that is maintaining the relationship no matter how much it costs. How do I know? Because it already cost Him the blood of His Son Jesus. His mercy and His love are so great that it renews each day that passes. So, no matter how you have messed up or how many days it has been since your last walk or talk, get back to your journey with God. He is waiting for you every morning. Thank Him this day for His forgiving forgetfulness, for how patient He is with you, and for His choice to reset every time you mess up. He still wants to walk with you every day … no matter what.

Naida M. Parson, Ph.D

63 DIRECT MY FOOTSTEPS

"Direct my footsteps according to Your word; let no sin rule over me. Redeem me from human oppression, that I may obey Your precepts. Make Your face shine on Your servant and teach me Your decrees. Streams of tears flow from my eyes, for Your law is not obeyed."

– Psalm 119:133-136 (NIV)

The key to the Enoch Experience of walking with God is being able to stay in step with Him. Its moving when He moves and stopping when He stops. If you feel Him stepping towards prayer, you pray. If you're saying something and you feel that tugging that He has stopped moving in the direction your mouth is going, then you stop talking. Walking with God means matching Him step by step on a daily basis.

Staying in step, however, is the hardest part. According to this scripture, one problem is sin. We are drawn to it, and honestly, we like it. Another problem is human relationships. The oppression of others causes us to lose focus on our relationship with God. Going through stressful times at work, or at home, or even at church can cause us to misstep. These issues threaten our ability to keep our steps aligned with God.

The writer of this psalm recognizes that he needs God to direct his steps according to God's word. He is heartbroken over his failure to obey the precepts of God. He realizes he needs God to light the way. He needs God to teach him how to do this walk. And so do all of us who are walking with Him now. As we study and learn the word of God, we can also ask Him how it can be done. Again, this is the hardest part, but our love for Him makes us fight every day to line our steps up with what God says in His word, the Holy Bible. It can be done through a prayer like this one, and by the power of the very word we are trying to stay in step with. Pray today for God to order or direct your steps in His word. Find more word to read today, and let its power keep you walking with God.

64 THERE IS A SACRIFICE

"Jesus answered, "If you want to be perfect, go, sell your possessions, and give to the poor, and you will have treasure in heaven. Then come, follow Me." When the young man heard this, he went away sad, because he had great wealth."

– Matthew 19:21-22 (NIV)

What an opportunity it is to be chosen to walk with God! We are not worthy, but He counted us worthy because of the sacrifice of Jesus Christ. When we walk with God, we do so because He wanted relationship with us so badly that He sent Jesus to live a worthy life for us and then take our punishment for being sinful. He solved our sin problem and reconciled us to God. We can walk with God like Jesus did, with His rightness being counted as our rightness.

There is nothing we could have done to earn this privilege, but there is a sacrifice that goes with it. Some will consider this too hard and lose courage. The rich young ruler is an example of this. He was given an opportunity to join Jesus in His earthly mission. He was given an invitation to follow Him. He was asked to walk with the Savior of the world! The problem was that he couldn't take his money with him. He had to demonstrate that his heart was with Jesus and not with his money. The only way to keep in step in our walk with God is to want it more than you want all the things that distract you and take you off path. The rich young ruler couldn't do it. It was too much of a challenge. It was too great of a sacrifice. It was too much of a life changer. He chose what was easier for him and lost the opportunity of his life … of his eternal life.

Some may feel that this close and intimate walk with God is too difficult. Some may even consider this kind of walk somewhat overboard. If you truly believe in Jesus and accept Him as your Savior, you can go to heaven out of step (or can you?). It's not mine to judge how closely you have to walk with God to be considered in relationship with Him. You might be okay to go to heaven, but that's the only place you will go. God has so much available for you if you would only make the sacrifice, refuse to be distracted, and obey Him at every turn. Determine today to do whatever it takes to stay in step with God. Is there anything you are having a hard time giving up? If so, confess it today and determine to follow more closely than ever.

Naida M. Parson, Ph.D

65 OH, THE PLACES YOU'LL GO!

"The LORD had said to Abram, "Go from your country, your people and your father's household to the land I will show you. "I will make you into a great nation, and I will bless you; I will make your name great, and you will be a blessing. I will bless those who bless you, and whoever curses you I will curse; and all peoples on earth will be blessed through you." So, Abram went, as the LORD had told him ...

– Genesis 12:1-4a (NIV)

I want God to take me places! I want to see amazing things. I'm curious as to what He has in store for me. I want God to take me places! Places where His glory is revealed. Places where His power is expressed. Places where His kingdom is expanded and where miracles happen. I want God to take me places! Places where my mind is blown by His wisdom and creativity. Places where I am met with favor because He is with me.

Abram was one who walked with a God who wanted to take him places. Places he had never been, but he would be blessed there and would be a blessing to every nation in the world. Abram was headed to a promised land where God would establish him as a nation. The plan was that Jesus Christ would come through his genetic line and thereby bless the entire world. Abram was just one person in a greater eternal plan, but in order for him to be in the right place at the right time, he had to walk with God.

You are also one person in a greater eternal plan. Your walk with God has purpose. He wants to use your life to bless others and have an eternal impact on their lives. Like Abram, you have been chosen to play a part, but you must get from where you are to where your blessing, your destiny, and your purpose is established and waiting. You will thrive in what He has for you. He will bless you, if you go. He will establish you, if you go. He will cause you to be a blessing, if you will only go where God wants to take you. Decide to continue in obedience today and get excited about it. Of course, it's all for His glory, but He will have a little something in it for you, too.

66 AGREED

"Do two walk together unless they have agreed to do so?"

— Amos 3:3 (NIV)

It is impossible for two people to walk together unless there is an agreement on the direction they are going. They may not agree on whether it's the right path, the best path, or the easiest path. They don't have to. All they have to do is agree that this is the path they are taking, and both of them make the choice to go down it together. One may go by request and the other by consent, but each must put one foot in front of the other beside the one with whom they have decided to walk. Unless one is bound, and gagged, and forced onto his feet (that's not walking together anyway), there is a willingness of both parties to take steps at the same time in the same direction.

Walking with God requires your agreement. Once either of you is going in a direction away from the other, the walking together ends. We stay in agreement with God through prayer. Our prayer time is the place where agreements are made. We come to God daily in humble submission to His will and His way. We find out what He wants from us. We read His word to know His heart. We confess our sins and ask Him to forgive us for stepping outside of the path He has laid for us. We agree that He is forever right and that any desire we have, that is not reflective of His revealed truth, is entirely wrong.

Today, stay in step with God by going to Him in prayer and submitting your will to His. Make a commitment today to stay on the path He has determined is for your good. This may include making some major changes, staying with a diet, ending some relationships, or curbing some habits. This might mean increasing your prayer time, reading more scripture, or spending more time in ministry. Or, it could mean an adjustment in an attitude, or a shift in your thought processes. And it's not a one-shot deal, either. We come into agreement with God every day by prayer. By talking with Him. Since you can't see Him to stay in step with Him, you have to pray to know where He is and agree to be there with Him.

Naida M. Parson, Ph.D

67 ALONE WITH GOD

"But Jesus often withdrew to lonely places and prayed."

– Luke 5:16 (NIV)

Quiet time with God yields the greatest return in your walk with Him. This is your time to talk to Him and ask Him questions. It's your time to make your requests and wait before Him for answers. It's your time to reconnect, repent, be restored, be renewed, and be refilled. Quiet time is where relationship happens. It's where your friendship with God is developed. It's where you abide in Christ. Quiet time is where you are corrected and forgiven, enlightened and encouraged. It's the stuff God encounters are made of.

Your quiet time with God can be anytime you can pull away alone. Jesus made a habit of pulling away from the crowds to spend time with His Father. The Bible says, in other places, that His time was early in the mornings. Whatever time works for you, it's great to choose a place and prepare it. Get your coffee, or tea, or water. Get tissue in case there is a sneeze, or a runny nose, or tears. Your Bible should be there as God moves on your heart to read or look up a scripture as an answer to your prayer, or request. And, of course, bring your devotionals, or the current book you are reading. A journal, or notepad, and a pen would be perfect to jot down things that are revealed to you. Once you are in your place, there should be no reason to move until your quality time with God is done.

If you have not prepared such a place, do it today. If you don't have a specific time, choose one today. If sitting quietly doesn't work for you, then maybe a literal walk, or a quiet drive may suit you better, though that makes it hard to stop, and read, and record what God shares with you. The important thing is that you enjoy quiet time with God daily. It's the stuff intimacy with God is made of.

68 LEARNING HIS VOICE

"The LORD said, "Go out and stand on the mountain in the presence of the LORD, for the LORD is about to pass by." Then a great and powerful wind tore the mountains apart and shattered the rocks before the LORD, but the LORD was not in the wind. After the wind there was an earthquake, but the LORD was not in the earthquake. After the earthquake came a fire, but the LORD was not in the fire. And after the fire came a gentle whisper. When Elijah heard it, he pulled his cloak over his face and went out and stood at the mouth of the cave. Then a voice said to him, "What are you doing here, Elijah?""

— 1 Kings 19:11-13 (NIV)

There is much controversy in Christendom as to whether God speaks to mankind directly anymore. Many believe that now that the Bible is established, God only speaks to us through His written word. Other Christian leaders and teachers believe that God does speak to us, but only at pivotal moments in our lives when a major decision needs to be made, or a destiny moment is about to be missed. Still others believe that God speaks only in impressions in our spirit, while some claim to have actually heard His audible voice.

All I can share is my experience, and in my walk with God, I have learned the sound of His voice. I've never heard His audible voice, but I know He has one. Jesus heard it. Paul heard it. Moses heard it. Abraham heard it. And Elijah heard it, too. It was a pivotal time in his life and ministry. Elijah was in desperate need of encouragement and instruction. He experienced a great wind, but God was not in the wind. He then encountered a great earthquake, but God was not in the shaking of the earth. Then there was fire, and we know God has spoken through fire before. But not this time. This time God was in a gentle whisper … a still small voice. And Elijah knew it was Him.

Learn the sound of His voice. I have no idea how He will speak to you. I do know that it will always be in alignment with the written word of God, but there are other ways you will hear from Him. I dare not put God in a box. He has been known to speak through a rooster, and a donkey, an angel, and a ghost. He speaks through a perception, an instant understanding, an impression by the Holy Spirit into your spirit, or through a prophet, or a pastor, or a parent, or a friend. He may send a message through a song, or through a sign. But God knows how to speak to us plainly and in a way that we know it is Him. Pray for the ability to hear Him in whatever way He chooses to reveal Himself. That's the best way to stay in step.

Naida M. Parson, Ph.D

69 A CHANGE OF HEART

"The king's heart is in the hand of the Lord, like the rivers of water: He turns it wherever He wishes."

— Proverbs 21:1 (NKJV)

When you endeavor to stay in step with God, there will be times when your heart is turned away from Him. Distractions of life, sin, your own fleshly nature, relationships, work, money, and other passions all compete with your walk with God. But, when you return to Him daily in prayer, or after a bit of an absence from Him, it's most likely because He has His hand on your heart. Even if we haven't strayed, to stay in step and walk in the Spirit, sometimes our heart must be put in check. It must be turned in the right direction.

This proverb says that the heart of the king, meaning those in authority, is in the hand of God. This gives us comfort in knowing that there is One greater than any earthly leader Who is so very much in charge that He can turn the heart of a king any way He wishes. It's just like water being channeled in the direction of choice from the one who controls the flow. So, would not the same be possible for us who walk with Him? If we never hear His voice, we can take comfort in the fact that He holds our hearts in His hand and He can steer us from there.

Learn the impression of God's hand on your heart. Know when He is turning it and submit to His will. Does God desire to change your heart toward your spouse, your children, your job, a ministry, or the city you live in? Is God changing your heart about what you eat, or is He turning it away from sinful habits? Again, learn to know the feel of God pulling at your heart to turn it the way He wants it to go. You don't have to fear failure or falling prey to the Devil's schemes to lure you away from God. Your heart is in His hand, and He knows how to turn it. You must learn how to yield. Pray today for those areas in your life where you need a change of heart. Ask God to teach you how to know His hand and how to allow your heart to turn.

70 FORSAKE YOUR THOUGHTS AND RECEIVE HIS

"Let the wicked forsake their ways and the unrighteous their thoughts. Let them turn to the LORD, and He will have mercy on them, and to our God, for He will freely pardon. "For My thoughts are not your thoughts, neither are your ways My ways," declares the LORD. "As the heavens are higher than the earth, so are My ways higher than your ways and My thoughts than your thoughts."

– Isaiah 55:7-9 (NIV)

Our quiet time with God is the best time to have our thinking corrected and changed. We walk better with God when we think like He thinks. When we allow His thoughts to be our thoughts, and His ways to be our ways, we are in harmony with Him and that's really all walking with God is: being in harmony with Him daily.

In this scripture, Isaiah admonishes the wicked to forsake their ways and the unrighteous to forsake their thoughts. The reason wicked ways and unrighteous thoughts need to be forsaken is because they do not match God's ways and thoughts. So different are our human thoughts and ways than God's thoughts and ways, that God says they are as far apart as the heavens are to the earth. We can't touch the heavens from the earth and our thoughts can't touch God's thoughts. But that's not the end of the story. The gap is not impossible to cross. If we forsake our ways and thoughts, we can take on those high thoughts of God.

Learn the intrusion of His thoughts on your thoughts. This is how it works. As you spend time with God, His Holy Spirit will place in your born-again human spirit wisdom from the mind of God. It will intrude upon your unrighteous thoughts and replace them. As He replaces your thoughts, you are to embrace the new thoughts and accept them as your own. As you pray and spend your quiet time with God today, listen for the intrusion of God's thoughts over your thoughts. Instantly forsake yours and receive His and continue to walk humbly with Him.

Naida M. Parson, Ph.D

71   "SUB"MISSION

"In all your ways submit to Him, and He will make your paths straight."

– Proverbs 3:6 (NIV)

Submission. Why is it that we don't like that word? I like to think that it's because we were created to have dominion over the earth and everything in it. So submitting to anything isn't in our nature. That may be true for our human nature, but the answer most likely lies in our sinful nature. Submission means not getting our way. It means bowing our will to another and denying ourselves of what we want. It means not being the center of your own world.

Submission. I see two words there. "Sub" and "mission." "Sub" comes from the Latin word meaning "under." It means below, beneath, or lesser. The word submission then, means that my mission is under, below, beneath, or lessor than another's. When I submit, I'm agreeing to take the lower position. My wants, desires and plans certainly have a mission for me. But the mission God has for me is superior, more important, and even more desired. Consequently, my life is a life of submission. Walking with God means going His way despite the way I want to go.

Know today that God has a mission that involves your life, your gifts, your talents, and your resources. Though He often gives us what we want, and always what we need, His mission must take priority. Decide today that you will live a life of submission. Listen again for His guidance and submit to Him in all your ways. ALL of them. The path of your life will get straighter and straighter. You will waste less time. You will stay in step. You will experience more success than you could imagine. You'll begin to love the word "sub"mission, in spite of your human nature.

72 WE'RE THE WIFE IN THIS RELATIONSHIP

"Now as the church submits to Christ, so also wives should submit to their husbands in everything. Husbands, love your wives, just as Christ loved the church and gave Himself up for her

This is a profound mystery—but I am talking about Christ and the church. However, each one of you also must love his wife as he loves himself, and the wife must respect her husband."

– Ephesians 5:24-25, 32-33 (NIV)

Walking with God means submitting to His will and His way ... daily. Submission becomes your lifestyle. It is the way you express your love for God. It is the hallmark of your relationship with Him. Paul describes it like a traditional marriage in his day. In a male dominated society, it was an easy illustration. He was actually teaching on Christian marriage, but I want to draw your attention to how we walk with God. Basically, whether you're male or female in real life, you're the wife in the relationship. He is the Husband.

Jesus, God the Son, loved you so much that He gave Himself totally for you. He gave up His throne, His glory, and His place in heaven to come to earth and give His life, so that His life and blood would be exchanged for yours. He paid the penalty for your sins so that you could enter a relationship with Him and the Father for eternity. He is married to you, and as your Husband, He is the leader of the family. He is the priest, the provider, the protector, and the lover, just like a husband is supposed to be.

Your part is to simply follow His leadership and reverence and respect Him, just like the wife was instructed to do for her husband. Whatever you feel about marital roles is not my point, though the Bible is clear. Jesus wants marriage to reflect His relationship with the church. It's the latter relationship we want to learn about here. We are to live in submission to Jesus like we are the wife in the relationship. This may be quite a challenge to the men reading this book, but think of it this way. Christ wants you to trust His leadership in the same way you would want your wife to trust yours. Trust Him with the leadership of your life. So, ladies and gentlemen, humble yourselves even more today. Ask Him what He requires of you. Do it like a wife who is so in love, and so well taken care of, that it's absolutely no problem to reverence, and respect, and submit to the one who has given up his life for her.

Naida M. Parson, Ph.D

73 WE'RE THE SON IN THIS RELATIONSHIP

"My son, do not despise the LORD's discipline, and do not resent His rebuke, because the LORD disciplines those He loves, as a father the son he delights in."

– Proverbs 3:11-12 (NIV)

God is relational. He wants a family. Jesus, in showing us who God is, almost exclusively referred to Him as The Father. As you continue your walk with God, you must accept that you're the son. (Now, this one may be easier for our male readers). He is the Father. He sets the pace for the family. He determines the direction the family is going. He lays out the vision for the family and your job, as the son, is to follow directions. A son trusts that the father has his best interests in mind and that the father sees things that the son does not see or understand.

But because the son is a growing, self-willed, and free willed individual, maintaining the relationship will often require discipline. When we are going in the wrong direction, and when we make bad choices, it is the father's responsibility to correct us. Some of our mistakes are age appropriate. Because of our immaturity, we just don't know any better and our father teaches us what is right and wrong. Sometimes, we are just out right rebellious and do things we know are wrong, simply because we want to. Then our father must correct us more harshly, so we don't self-destruct.

Do not resent it when you are under the correction of God. This may come in the form of a rebuke (meaning a verbal condemnation of what you are doing). You may see it in the word of God, or hear it in a sermon, in prayer, or from a godly leader or friend. It may come in the form of trouble, or failure, or a painful loss of the thing you were chasing after that was not in God's will for you. In whatever way correction and discipline comes, you are to accept it as a son would from a father, line yourself back up with His will, and love Him the more for setting you straight. Today, ask God to correct your ways. It will certainly be in your best interest.

74 WE'RE THE PLAYER IN THIS RELATIONSHIP

"Praise be to the LORD my Rock, who trains my hands for war, my fingers for battle."

— Psalm 144:1 (NIV)

The idea of total submission and obedience to God in our walk with Him can be compared to a coach and a player on his team. God is the coach. You are the player. When a player respects and trusts his coach, he obeys instructions he may not understand himself. He may not see the purpose or the process, but he believes that if he walks step by step with his coach, he will be at peak performance, and perhaps come out a champion. He trusts two things; that the coach knows him, and that the coach knows the game.

David was a warrior and a worshipper. He was famous for winning battles for Israel. But he didn't give himself the credit for being gifted or smart. He lets us know what made him good at what he was called to do. He gave praise to God Whom he called his Rock. This is interesting because David's most famous victory was accomplished with a rock. He lets us know Who the true Rock was that day, his Coach. God is the One who trained David's hands to war. David assumed the position of a player on God's team and allowed God to instruct him, train him, teach him, and bring the best out of him.

In this relationship with God, He is not merely a consultant or advice giver. He is a commander. He is an instructor. He is the final authority. He knows you and He knows this thing He created that we call life. He knows economics and politics, psychology and anatomy, love and romance, marriage and parenthood. Let Him coach you in every area of your life today. He will bring you to peak performance and you'll win some championships along the way.

Naida M. Parson, Ph.D

75 DON'T LET SIN SEPARATE YOU

"Surely the arm of the Lord is not too short to save, nor His ear too dull to hear. But your iniquities have separated you from your God; your sins have hidden His face from you, so that He will not hear."

– Isaiah 59:1-2 (NIV)

The key to walking with God is to stay close. Sin, however, separates us from God. Before the sacrifice of Jesus on the cross, God and humankind had irreconcilable differences. The problem between us was sin. Sin is missing the mark, meaning the standard God has set for human behavior, thought, and feeling. Sin is a transgression against the law of God. It's any disobedience or rebellion against His will for our lives. It's knowing the right or good thing to do and choosing not to do it. God hates sin. We love it. God won't live with it. We won't live without it. God turns His face from it. We run to it. God can't embrace it. We can't let it go. Irreconcilable differences caused a separation between us and God.

Even though Jesus has taken away our sin at the cross, it still has an impact on our relationship with God. When we sin, we tend to pull away from Him. We don't want to pray or come near Him. In the midst of our wrongdoing, we may even pretend that God doesn't exist for a moment. We try not to be cognizant that He is right there with us, watching us choose our own pleasure over our relationship with Him. As I stated before, when you block God out of your mind to purposely commit a sin, it's like being an atheist just for a moment, because at that point you wish that He didn't exist!

Isaiah is telling Israel that God has not lost the power to save them, but their sins have separated them from Him and as long as they choose this rebellious lifestyle, God would not hear them. It is God's will that we live a life that reflects we are walking with Him. The Apostle Paul calls this "walking worthy." Paul says that just because Jesus has paid the price for our sins by His grace, we shouldn't continue to live in sin. We should behave as if we are dead to it and end our love affair with it. Examine your life today for anything you are still doing, thinking, or feeling that interrupts your relationship with God. Ask Him to cleanse you from it and take it out of your life. Reconcile your differences. Today.

76 STAY CLOSE BY NOT HURTING HIM

"I will sing for the One I love a song about His vineyard: My loved One had a vineyard on a fertile hillside. He dug it up and cleared it of stones and planted it with the choicest vines. He built a watchtower in it and cut out a winepress as well. Then He looked for a crop of good grapes, but it yielded only bad fruit. "Now you dwellers in Jerusalem and people of Judah, judge between Me and My vineyard. What more could have been done for My vineyard than I have done for it? When I looked for good grapes, why did it yield only bad? Now I will tell you what I am going to do to My vineyard: I will take away its hedge, and it will be destroyed; I will break down its wall, and it will be trampled. I will make it a wasteland, neither pruned nor cultivated, and briers and thorns will grow there. I will command the clouds not to rain on it." The vineyard of the LORD Almighty is the nation of Israel, and the people of Judah are the vines He delighted in. And He looked for justice, but saw bloodshed; for righteousness, but heard cries of distress."

– Isaiah 5:1-7 (NIV)

When we do things that hurt and grieve God, especially things done disrespectfully in His face, it causes distance between us and God. Our endeavor in walking with Him is to stay close to Him. So, we want to be diligent about getting rid of anything that displeases Him. He has given us everything we need to live righteously. He has forgiven our sins, given us a spiritual nature, filled us with the power of the Holy Spirit, and has given us His word to read and study so we can purify our ways.

Isaiah is speaking to the children of Israel and the inhabitants of Judah when he gives this analogy of one who has planted a vineyard. The ground was fertile and prepared for choice vines to be planted. So great was the planter's expectation that He built a tower to watch and protect it, and a winepress to make wine from the crop. But, despite all his efforts, only bad grapes were produced. He is so angry and outdone that he destroys the vineyard. The story shows more than anger. It shows hurt. He asks, "what more could I have done for it?"

If you're reading this book, God has been more than good to you. Don't let a love affair with your old ways continue to hurt the God that has done everything He could to bring you to a blessed and

Naida M. Parson, Ph.D

productive life. He is looking for good grapes. Make sure He gets them. Continue daily to weed out of your life everything that is hurtful to God. He deserves it. Pray now for Him to reveal anything about you that is hurtful to Him. Remember God is relational, and you mean everything to Him. Honor that by showing that He means everything to you as well.

77 STAY CLOSE BY OBEYING HIM

""If you love Me, keep My commands.

Whoever has My commands and keeps them is the one who loves Me. The one who loves Me will be loved by My Father, and I too will love them and show Myself to them."

Jesus replied, "Anyone who loves Me will obey My teaching. My Father will love them, and We will come to them and make Our home with them. Anyone who does not love Me will not obey My teaching. These words you hear are not My own; they belong to the Father who sent Me."

– John 14:15, 21, 23-24 (NIV)

"If you love Me keep My commands" is another relational concept Jesus teaches that should govern our walk with Him. Loving Him is not the mushy feelings and deep-felt affection we associate with being in love, although you will feel that, too. Loving God is found in obeying His commands. If you think about our earthly relationships, if someone loves you they don't continue to do in your face what brings you so much pain. If someone loves you, they don't like to see you hurting. So, you would say, "if you love me, don't keep doing that."

You don't stay close to anything that keeps hurting you, so it is difficult to continue a loving walk with God when you keep doing things that hurt Him. Sometimes I think we are just fond of God. We think He's a nice guy and we enjoyed meeting Him. But do we really love Him? Do we really want to do whatever it takes to stay close to Him? Jesus says that the way to be in a love relationship with He and the Father is to live a life obedient to His commands. This sounds strange to us because we wouldn't expect to have to live in total obedience to the ones we love on earth. That's not love. That's domination and control. But remember, you and God are not equals. You're the submissive wife in this relationship. He is the Husband who gave His total self for you. You're the son who is totally dependent on the Father. You're the player whose peak performance is only reached as he obeys his Coach.

Today, put yourself in the place of a child who loves his or her parent so much that they honor them by following the house rules, doing their chores, and coming home on time. No parent feels loved

Naida M. Parson, Ph.D

and respected because the kid says it every day or even sings it in a song. The parent feels loved when the children obey their commands. Our God is no different. Our Lord Jesus is no different. The Holy Spirit is no different. Love is not a feeling to them. It's a decision made daily to stay close and walk with them in humble obedience.

78 STAY CLOSE THROUGH PRAYER

"The LORD is near to all who call on Him, to all who call on Him in truth."

– Psalm 145:18 (NIV)

Prayer helps you stay close to God. Prayer is not just talking to God, or at God. Prayer is conversation WITH God. Actually, prayer comes in many forms. There is thanksgiving where you tell Him what you are thankful for. There is praise and worship where you declare your awe of what He has done and your appreciation of Who He is. There is intercession where you pray for others, and supplication where you ask for what you need. There is declaration where you speak things into the atmosphere with your God given authority, and let's not forget spiritual warfare where you bind, rebuke, and cast out demons. Prayer is also where you commit things to Him and receive instruction and revelation from Him.

All of these forms of prayer cause Him to draw nearer to you. But remember that you and God are in a relationship. You should have times that you ask Him about things that don't have anything to do with church, or ministry, or other people, or your personal needs. No one likes to be in a relationship where the only conversation is about what the other person needs, or about the business at hand. Have some prayer time that's not about you at all.

Today, ask God to do more of the talking than you do. Ask Him a question about what is on His heart. Ask Him to show you parts of Him that you haven't experienced. He has called us friends. Practice having a friend conversation today. If you don't know His voice, ask anyway like you're writing a letter to a friend. He knows how to reveal Himself to you, and He certainly will be thrilled that you want to know Him and not just what He can do for you. Praying in this way will help you get close and stay close as you walk humbly with your God.

Naida M. Parson, Ph.D

79 ASK HIM ABOUT HIM

"It is the glory of God to conceal a matter; to search out a matter is the glory of kings."

— Proverbs 25:2 (NIV)

"The disciples came to Him and asked, "Why do You speak to the people in parables?" He replied, "Because the knowledge of the secrets of the kingdom of heaven has been given to you, but not to them."

— Matthew 13:10-11 (NIV)

God is a mystery to mankind. That's what makes Him God. If we understood everything about Him, and could decipher His every move and decision, He would cease to be God. But that doesn't mean He is opposed to us knowing Him as intimately as is humanly possible. He longs to be known by His children. He sent Jesus Christ into the world, not just to die for us, but also to make the Father known to us. It is the glory of God that He is so mysterious and above us, but it is ours to seek Him out and know Him in new and exciting ways.

Jesus had a group of inner circle followers who had the opportunity to know things that others weren't given the privilege to know. He spoke to everyone else in parables, but for His disciples He opened the very secrets of the Kingdom of Heaven. There are some secret things God will share with those who follow Him closely and want to know Him. You don't have to be anyone you would consider special. There was nothing special about a bunch of fishermen, working class guys, and a few rebels. There was nothing special about Enoch, either whose experience we are chasing. You can walk with God, and He will show you some things, and take you places you can't imagine.

Ask Him about Him again today. Ask Him about the purpose of animals. Ask Him what bothers Him, or what He is concerned about in this season. Ask Him what He sees in you, what He wants from you, and how you can please Him even more. Ask Him what you can do to be closer to Him and maybe even see if He will tell you a secret or two. I know some may think this is weird or dangerous, but you're not trying to fake up a new revelation or start a new religion. You may not even get a clear answer. It's the loving intimacy we are after. So go to Him. He is waiting.

80 COME LET US WORSHIP

"O come, let us sing unto the Lord: let us make a joyful noise to the Rock of our salvation. Let us come before His presence with thanksgiving and make a joyful noise unto Him with psalms. For the Lord is a great God, and a great King above all gods. In His hand are the deep places of the earth: the strength of the hills is His also. The sea is His, and He made it: and His hands formed the dry land. O come, let us worship and bow down: let us kneel before the Lord our Maker."

– Psalms 95:1-6 (KJV)

Worship helps you stay close to God. In worship you can get mushy with Him, tell Him how you feel about Him, be vulnerable in His presence, and express your adoration. Worship is more intimate than praise. It's more about how you feel about God personally than what you feel about the things He has done. Worship grows deeper as your relationship with God becomes more intimate. It may start with just acknowledging Who He is and expressing that to Him. The next level would be ritualistic or religious service to Him because of Who He is. Then, as you experience more life with Him, your worship of Him begins to change your lifestyle and you become more and more like Him. The highest level of worship is when your yielding to His will becomes an unconditional, continual yes.

But it all starts with the realization of how worthy He is. How important He is. Worship comes from "worth-ship" and in the Bible worth, or worthy, often meant "of full weight." If something measured its full expected weight, it was deemed "worthy." The Psalmist here speaks of the greatness of God as the King above all. The earth, and the seas, and the hills are all in His hands and made by His hands. He is of full weight. He is all He claims to be. He is worthy. No matter what may be happening in your life, or in the world, nothing can take away the fact that God is worthy of our praise and our worship.

Work on your worship today. Take some time to just adore God for Who He is. Tell Him Who He is in the universe, Who He is in heaven and earth, and ultimately Who He is to you. Take time to just sit in His presence. You may play worship music or play your own instrument for Him. You may just sit quietly in a beautiful place He created admiring His work. You may just express your love from your heart. However you choose, do it often. Do it daily. Even if it is awkward at first. You'll get the hang of it. It will keep you close.

Naida M. Parson, Ph.D

81 WORK WITH HIM

"Jesus gave them this answer: "Very truly I tell you, the Son can do nothing by Himself; He can do only what He sees His Father doing, because whatever the Father does the Son also does. For the Father loves the Son and shows Him all He does. Yes, and He will show Him even greater works than these, so that you will be amazed."

– John 5:19-20 (NIV)

In order to have a great and close walking relationship with God, we must pray, worship, obey Him, and make Him a priority in our lives. Another way to develop this close relationship is to work alongside Him. Many times, the people we are closest to are our coworkers. We go through life together, eat together, grow together, and bond with each other, especially if our jobs are dangerous and/or require long hours, extra teamwork, and social support.

It's the same with God. Working together and being involved in His activities helps you stay close to Him. You share in His burden for the world, and in His joy when His plans and purposes are accomplished. This is the kind of closeness He had with His Son, Jesus. Jesus said He didn't do anything by Himself. He only did what He saw His Father doing. His power and authority came from God. When He saw where His Father was moving, He joined in and worked alongside Him. And, wow, did They do amazing things together! Jesus based that on the love relationship They had. Their closeness resulted in great works, and Their great work together resulted in Their continued closeness.

It works that way for us, too. Jesus said if we would abide in Him, stay close to Him, so close we are actually *in* Him, we would do greater works than even He did with His Father. This doesn't always mean things we do through the church or a formal ministry. We can work with Him every day in our homes, on our jobs, at school, or anywhere there are people He wants to impact. Share some of the joy of working with your Savior today. Pray and see who He is working on near you and join in and work with Him. Doing this daily will give you and God another level of closeness.

82 JUST BE WITH HIM

"Jesus went up on a mountainside and called to Him those He wanted, and they came to Him. He appointed twelve that they might be with Him and that He might send them out to preach"

— Mark 3:13-14 (NIV)

What a great scripture this is when it comes to walking with God! Jesus is about to begin His public ministry and He goes up on a mountainside to pray. During that prayer, I believe He and the Father discussed one of the most important decisions ever made in the universe. Who are the 12 leaders to be trained by Jesus Christ Himself and left to begin the New Testament church? He chose them to send them to preach. But that was secondary. First, they were chosen to be with Him.

For the next 3 years or so, they would all experience life with Jesus. They would walk with Him, go to weddings, and dinners, and funerals with Him (though He tended to wreck funerals by raising the dearly departed from the dead), eat with Him, sleep with Him, and minister to people all over the region. In between, He would teach them things, show them things, and allow them to experience things they could not have imagined. This is walking with God at its best!

Experience life together with God. That means work, relationships, vacations, school, hard times, good times, birthdays, parenthood, marriage, ministry, illness, tragedy, and triumphs. And, of course, everything in between. While all that is going on, He will teach you things and take you places both spiritually and naturally. God wants to experience life with you. He wants to be the central part of your life, and He invites you to be in His. Take time today and invite God into your daily life. Ask Him about your daily things. Get His advice about your everyday issues. He wants in! Every day.

Naida M. Parson, Ph.D

83 MAKE GOD YOUR PRIORITY

"Do not worship any other god, for the LORD, whose name is Jealous, is a jealous God."

– Exodus 34:14 (NIV)

"Anyone who loves their father or mother more than Me is not worthy of Me; anyone who loves their son or daughter more than Me is not worthy of Me."

– Matthew 10:37 (NIV)

The Old Testament teaches us that God is a jealous God. He will not share His position as God with anyone, especially a false, man-made god. As Jesus comes on the scene, being God in the flesh, He demands the same priority. If you are going to walk with God in a way that pleases Him, you will have to make this relationship your priority.

This relationship must be first. Priority comes from the word prior. God must be before anything else and anyone else. He becomes your first thought in the morning and your resting place at night. He must be your first response and not your last resort. Every life decision is filtered through His will. Every victory is shared with Him because it's because of Him. Every disappointment is shared with Him because you submit to His will. You always choose Him first. Nothing gets in the way of your relationship. Your complete loyalty is to Him.

Be intentional today about making this relationship with God your priority. Give Him first position in your life by looking at your schedule and seeing if it reflects that He holds that position. Give Him priority. Sometimes the one who is in first position doesn't always get priority treatment. Make sure that God gets as much energy and time as is due someone who is of utmost importance to you. Make your choices today based on what makes Him happy above the interests of anyone or anything else. This is how you walk with God.

84 SHOW GOD HE IS PRIORITY

"A woman in that town who lived a sinful life learned that Jesus was eating at the Pharisee's house, so she came there with an alabaster jar of perfume. As she stood behind Him at His feet weeping, she began to wet His feet with her tears. Then she wiped them with her hair, kissed them and poured perfume on them. When the Pharisee who had invited Him saw this, he said to himself, "If this man were a prophet, He would know who is touching Him and what kind of woman she is—that she is a sinner."

Then He turned toward the woman and said to Simon, "Do you see this woman? I came into your house. You did not give me any water for My feet, but she wet My feet with her tears and wiped them with her hair. You did not give Me a kiss, but this woman, from the time I entered, has not stopped kissing My feet. You did not put oil on My head, but she has poured perfume on My feet."

– Luke 7:37-39, 44-46 (NIV)

How do you show someone they are your priority? Their time, their needs, and their wants are attended to before anyone else's, and without the distraction of anyone else's. You put most of your time, energy and money into their wants and needs at the expense of anyone who is not at that level of priority. If your walk with God, and your relationship with God, is truly your priority, you will attend to His time with you and resist any interruption. You will do the things He asks of you without procrastination. You will serve the Kingdom in the way He desires without argument or complaining.

Here in Luke, we find a contrast between two people. They were both interested in Jesus. They both wanted to know Him. They both even honored Him, but from two different angles and perspectives. Simon was part of the religious elite. He honored Jesus by bringing Him into his home. This said that Jesus was important because an important man invited Him in. The sinner woman came from a very different place. She most likely saw herself as nothing and saw Jesus as everything. She took the most expensive thing she may have had and poured it on Him. Simon may have felt He did well because he let Jesus in his home. The sinner woman was so grateful, to the point of tears, that Jesus would come to let her into His kingdom. Before it was over, her many sins had been forgiven and her faith had saved her.

Naida M. Parson, Ph.D

Find some way today to show God that He is your priority. Show Him how important He is in your life. What can you do to show Him you are grateful to be forgiven? Is there something you hold dear that can be given to Him or to His kingdom? Is there some act of service that you know would make Him smile? Or maybe, just some time spent in worship of Him that is not distracted or shared with any other activity or agenda of your own. Ask Him today, what is it that you have that can be poured on Him in gratitude and praise?

85   FROM FELLOWSHIP TO FRIENDSHIP TO PARTNERSHIP

"I want to know Christ—yes, to know the power of His resurrection and participation in His sufferings, becoming like Him in His death, and so, somehow, attaining to the resurrection from the dead. Not that I have already obtained all this, or have already arrived at my goal, but I press on to take hold of that for which Christ Jesus took hold of me. Brothers and sisters, I do not consider myself yet to have taken hold of it. But one thing I do: Forgetting what is behind and straining toward what is ahead, I press on toward the goal to win the prize for which God has called me heavenward in Christ Jesus."

– Philippians 3:10-14 (NIV)

The longer you walk in step with God, the more you will get to know Him. The goal is to build a relationship and let it evolve. Your relationship evolves from fellowship to friendship to partnership. You fellowship daily with a God you may not know very well. Your relationship is based on honor, respect, and reverence. Then, as life goes on and you experience some things together (sorrows, triumphs, challenges, and some boring days), you develop a friendship. He is your "go to" person for everything in life. He is your first response and not your last resort. Then, you catch His heart for people and the world, and you sense His calling on your life. It is then that you move into a partnership and fulfill His plan and purpose. This may be from raising children, to being a great spouse, to local ministry in your church and community, to worldwide mission, or all of the above.

Paul said it eloquently. He wanted to know Jesus. And he wanted his knowledge of Him to evolve. Paul wanted to know the power that raised Jesus from the dead. He knew that meant to participate in suffering like Jesus. To identify with His death meant to die to himself and his desires. And then he could know the new life that is found in God through Jesus Christ and at the end, be resurrected to eternal life where his Friend dwelt forever. Paul said he wasn't there, yet. He didn't know Jesus that intimately yet, but he was willing to put the past behind him and press with all he had to reach that goal of knowing Him and finishing out what he was called to do.

    Naida M. Parson, Ph.D

So today have joy in continuing this journey. Walk with Him. Talk with Him. Ask Him questions. Read about Him. Study who He is. Let Him in on everything you do. Share your day, your issues, your problems, your challenges, and your joys. Let Him reach out to you and show you through His word, and His presence, Who He is and Who He can be in your life. Enjoy your time with God today. Let the fellowship build into a friendship. Let the friendship build into a partnership. He is waiting for you, even now.

86 EVERY YEAR CLOSER, EVERY YEAR DEEPER

"His divine power has given us everything we need for a godly life through our knowledge of Him who called us by His own glory and goodness. Through these He has given us His very great and precious promises, so that through them you may participate in the divine nature, having escaped the corruption in the world caused by evil desires. For this very reason, make every effort to add to your faith goodness; and to goodness, knowledge; and to knowledge, self-control; and to self-control, perseverance; and to perseverance, godliness; and to godliness, mutual affection; and to mutual affection, love. For if you possess these qualities in increasing measure, they will keep you from being ineffective and unproductive in your knowledge of our Lord Jesus Christ."

— 2 Peter 1:3-8 (NIV)

The goal of walking humbly with your God is to know Him and to be in intimate, ongoing relationship with Him. Every year you should be closer. Your relationship should grow more intimate and your knowledge of Him should continue to grow. Your faith and trust in Him should be stronger and more automatic as the years go on. You should know Him so well that you never doubt Him, never question His existence, and never mistrust His judgment. This comes with years of walking with Him. Every year, closer. Every year, deeper.

The Apostle Peter writes that everything we need to live a godly life comes by our knowledge of Jesus Christ. The more we walk with Him and learn about Him, the more it changes our earthly sinful nature into a divine nature; a godly, spiritually excellent nature. This is a progressive process. It starts with saving faith, and then goodness, a change in our behavior. To goodness we add more knowledge of Him, and that knowledge leads to another change in behavior, self-control. Add to self-control, perseverance, the ability to hang in there and not quit. That will then lead to godliness, the ultimate behavior change. Your emotional life grows with it, and you mature from mutual love to unconditional love. Peter most likely didn't mean this to be an exclusive list of character and behavior, nor that this is the exact process for everyone. His point is that your knowledge of God grows, and adds virtue and behavior change at each level. The goal is to be effective and productive in your knowledge of Jesus Christ.

Naida M. Parson, Ph.D

So let today be a continuation of the process you are in. Continue to get to know the God you are serving. Let Him change something in your behavior. Or, perhaps something in your character needs to become more like Him. As you walk with Him today, ask Him to show you more about His character. Ask Him to reveal something about Himself that gives you a deeper understanding of who He is and what He wants for you, for His children, or for His world. Share with Him something deeper about you, even though He already knows. The conversation will build your relationship and your intimacy will grow deeper. Pray today for a closer walk with Him.

87 KEEP GROWING

"Therefore, let us move beyond the elementary teachings about Christ and be taken forward to maturity, not laying again the foundation of repentance from acts that lead to death, and of faith in God, instruction about cleansing rites, the laying on of hands, the resurrection of the dead, and eternal judgment. And God permitting, we will do so."

— Hebrews 6:1-3 (NIV)

The most natural thing in the world is to grow. We grow up. We grow out. We grow more mature. There is nothing we have to do to make that happen except to keep eating and breathing and moving. It's in our DNA to grow from an embryo, to a fetus, to an infant, to a toddler, to a child, a teen, an adult and so on. Unless something is wrong, we will naturally grow, change, and develop. The same happens with our knowledge of Jesus and our relationship in our walk with God. As long as we keep feeding on the word of God, breathing in His Spirit, and staying in step with Him, we will grow and mature in our knowledge of Him.

The writer of Hebrews is anxious to move on to deeper knowledge. He urges the believers to leave elementary school about Christ. The writer had been forced to repeat the basics of repentance, faith, what rituals to follow, what laying on hands was about, the resurrection and eternal life. All of them were good subjects and necessary, but there is so much more to learn about God. He is vast. He is fascinating. He is an experience. He holds the universe in His hand. He is amazing. He is wonderful. Do you know what that means? He is full of wonders! He is awe inspiring. And His word is powerfully alive. It speaks to you. It changes you. It reveals God to you in a supernatural way. You can read the same verse over again on a different day and it can speak to you in a totally different way. You can hear a sermon about the same story, and it touches you in a different way than it did last year. The impetus for this book was God saying to me that there is so much more to Him than church! He is the God of the universe and eternity beyond, and I had boiled Him down to just church.

Know more about Him. Grow in your knowledge of Him. Read more of His love letter to the world that we call the Bible. Walk with Him daily and drink of His Spirit. You do that by asking Him to continue to fill you with His Spirit, praising Him in word and song, worshipping Him in love and truth, resting in His presence and spending those quiet times with Him daily. Then look

Naida M. Parson, Ph.D

for more about Him. Study something you haven't studied before. Continue to ask Him questions about Himself and what He requires from your life. Let's leave elementary school, eventually. If you are early in your walk with God, you're okay where you are. Keep reading and feeding and you will grow. If you're older in God, let's move on to maturity.

88 JESUS IS EASY

"Come to Me, all you who are weary and burdened, and I will give you rest. Take My yoke upon you and learn from Me, for I am gentle and humble in heart, and you will find rest for your souls. For My yoke is easy and My burden is light."

— Matthew 11:28-30 (NIV)

Sometimes we make Christianity so hard. We make it so complicated that many Christians are full of fear. We are afraid of failing God. We are afraid of not completing our ministry assignments. We are afraid that we won't do things well enough. We live in the fear of not being good enough and we see God as an angry parent waiting to expose our bad behavior and punishing it when He does. Or maybe, just out of pure love for Him, we strive so hard to become what and who we believe He wants us to be. It's a noble cause, but an impossible one if we rely on our own ability. And so, we struggle, and strive, and feel bad way too much in our walk with God.

That is the opposite of what Jesus taught walking with God should be like. In our verses today, Jesus was talking to people who had already had a tough enough life. They were made to feel that the only way to please God was to follow a long list of laws, and failure to do so made them less than, unworthy, and unclean. They had become a nation of people far from God with no way of reaching Him. They were waiting on a Messiah who would make things right again. And here He was with a simple message. Learn of Me. Learn from Me. I am gentle, and humble in heart and you will find rest for your souls. Just come to Me. I will give rest to those who feel the weight of life and religion.

Jesus is easy. Take the time to learn more about Who God is. Know Who Jesus is. Know the working of the Holy Spirit in your life. You will find that this Christian walk is a lot easier than religion has made it. It does require some things. There are standards of behavior appropriate for Christians. There are ministry assignments to be done. But none of that is the basis for being loved and accepted by God. Learn of Him. You will find that the moment you accepted Jesus Christ as your personal Savior, you became everything God has ever wanted you to be. You are righteous in His Son, Jesus. When He looks at you, He sees His Son and He is pleased. It's that easy. Just walk with Him. Remain in Him. He will give you grace for all the rest. He will teach you and you will respond. Let your knowledge of Jesus give you rest today and learn something more about Him. Hopefully, you just did.

Naida M. Parson, Ph.D

89 KNOW HIM THROUGH HIS WORD

"Therefore, when Christ came into the world, He said: "Sacrifice and offering You did not desire, but a body You prepared for Me; with burnt offerings and sin offerings You were not pleased. Then I said, 'Here I am—it is written about Me in the scroll— I have come to do Your will, My God.""

– Hebrews 10:5-7 (NIV)

God is relational. He wants us to know Him. Adam and Eve were created to walk with God, to have relationship with Him, and to be an extension of His love. It's not much different than the desire some may have to parent children. They want a family to love and to relate to. They want a family to spend life with and to share joys. The children they have may not love them or share life with them the way they want them to, but everyday some human being takes that risk and has children anyway. God knew we would make choices that separated us from Him, but He created us anyway because … well, we may never understand why completely. But He wrote us a book by the inspiration of His Holy Spirit and through the Bible we are privy to the thoughts, the love, the knowledge, the attitudes, the passions, the desires, the commands, and the expectations of our Almighty Creator. The best way to know Him is through His written word.

We also know that Jesus Christ is called "The Word." We know God through His Son, Jesus Christ. The writer of Hebrews tells us that Jesus was sent into the world as the ultimate sacrifice for our sins against God. Because God knew our rebellion would separate us, He created a way for our sins to be forgiven so we could be in relationship with Him again while not violating His law which requires death for disobedience. Until Jesus came to pay the full penalty, God accepted burnt offerings and sin offerings. Now, only the offering up of Jesus' blood is required, and we have been restored to our right relationship with God. The writer goes on to say that this is what the entire Bible is all about. Every scripture written up to that time points to Jesus. And everything accepted as scripture after that time is also all about Jesus. From Genesis to Revelation, God lays out for us Who He is and introduces us to His Son and His Holy Spirit. The way to learn about God is to read His book. He reveals Himself through His word. The more you read it, the more you learn of Him, and the more you learn of Him, the more you know Him.

Have a more excited view of the Bible today. When you read it, find what it tells you about the character of God. Don't try to create an image of God from the perspective of people who don't know Him. God is not created in our image. We are created in His! We can't make Him what we want Him to be. We can't make Him do what we think He should do. We certainly can't judge if what He does, or what He allows, is good or bad, right, or wrong. Don't guess at what your God is like. Read the book. You may be surprised at Who He really is, how deeply He loves, and how great He reigns. Know Him through His Word. It's a sixty-six-book love letter to you. Read it.

90 KNOW HIM BY EXPERIENCING LIFE WITH HIM

"By faith Abraham, when called to go to a place he would later receive as his inheritance, obeyed and went, even though he did not know where he was going. By faith he made his home in the promised land like a stranger in a foreign country; he lived in tents, as did Isaac and Jacob, who were heirs with him of the same promise. For he was looking forward to the city with foundations, whose architect and builder is God. And by faith even Sarah, who was past childbearing age, was enabled to bear children because she considered Him faithful who had made the promise. And so, from this one man, and he as good as dead, came descendants as numerous as the stars in the sky and as countless as the sand on the seashore.

By faith Abraham, when God tested him, offered Isaac as a sacrifice. He who had embraced the promises was about to sacrifice his one and only son, even though God had said to him, "It is through Isaac that your offspring will be reckoned." Abraham reasoned that God could even raise the dead, and so in a manner of speaking he did receive Isaac back from death."

— Hebrews 11:8-12, 17-19 (NIV)

They say you never really know a person until you have lived with them. There is something about spending your life with a person that shows you who they are in multiple situations and through all kinds of seasons. People can be very different when they are in pain versus when all is well. You see the character of people when death happens, or they lose a job, or they have a great unexpected success. When you go through your own ups and downs, seasons and situations, you know better how people love you and how they support you... or not. Experience is said to be the best teacher there is and experiencing life with a person teaches you more about them than reading about them, or hearing stories from someone else's perspective.

Abraham is a great example of experiencing life with God. They started off on a journey together when God chose him to be the father of faith. Abraham was chosen to be the genetic line for Jesus Christ to come through. God sent him away from his family into a country he didn't know. They experienced moving, settling, working, wealth, marriage, infertility, baby mamma drama, marital conflict, disappointment, testing, famine, wars, loss, politics, covenants, promises, waiting, joy, ministry, raising kids, remarriage, adult child issues, and preparation for death. Abraham had intimacy with God. So much so, that when He was about to destroy two cities, He told the angels He couldn't hide it from Abraham. They knew each other. They trusted each other. They argued with each other. They experienced life together and they changed the world together.

Experiencing life with God is a great way to get to know Him. You find out more about His character, His love, His ability, and His judgement as you experience things and go through seasons. The first time someone close to you dies, you experience His ability to sustain and comfort. When you go through financial struggle, you learn of His ability to provide. When you sin a great sin, you learn of His forgiveness and grace. When you raise children with Him right there by your side, you learn of His wisdom and guidance. And when you're angry with Him because you don't understand something He allowed, you learn of His faithfulness and that there are things too deep for you to know. The Bible is filled with the experiences of others, and because the word of God is inspired by His Spirit, I have to believe it is the primary way to know Him. But having your own experiences with God will give you a knowledge of Him that is close up and personal. Let God be with you in everything you do today. Talk to Him about everything. Find out more about Him in good times, in bad times, and in those times you are just mad at life and maybe even at Him. He wants you to know Him. Experience really is the best teacher.

91 KNOW HIM THROUGH HIS SPIRIT

"However, as it is written: "What no eye has seen, what no ear has heard, and what no human mind has conceived" — the things God has prepared for those who love Him— these are the things God has revealed to us by His Spirit. The Spirit searches all things, even the deep things of God. For who knows a person's thoughts except their own spirit within them? In the same way no one knows the thoughts of God except the Spirit of God.

The person without the Spirit does not accept the things that come from the Spirit of God but considers them foolishness, and cannot understand them because they are discerned only through the Spirit."

— 1 Corinthians 2:9-11, 14 (NIV)

There are many ways bible scholars have attempted to explain, not only the triune nature of God, but the triune nature of mankind created in His image. One of those ways is this: man is a spirit, he has a soul, and he lives in a body. Man was made of the dust of the ground. God breathed into this lifeless dust. Breath is the biblical expression of spirit. God breathed into man "spirit", and man became a living soul. Our bodies connect us to the natural world. Our soul gives us self consciousness and connects the natural and the spiritual. But it is through our spirit that we are God connected. We are conscious of Him, we speak to Him, and we know Him through our spirit.

Paul explains that what our natural man cannot phantom, our spirit man knows. There are things that can only be revealed to us through our spirit. The Holy Spirit searches the deeper things of God. The Holy Spirit knows the thoughts of God because He is God's Spirit at work in the world. He is God's Spirit at work in us, helping us to know God, to experience Him, to understand Him, and to communicate with Him in a way that defies our understanding, that goes beyond our wisdom, and that reveals to us things in a deeper way than we could have ever known. The Bible says that a person without the Spirit would think the things of God are foolish. Some things can only be revealed to us Spirit to spirit.

Our walk with God is a spiritual walk. Our deeper knowledge of God comes through communion with His Holy Spirit. Ask the Holy Spirit to fill you today. Ask Him to reveal to you more about the

Father. Learn to listen in a different way. Make steps to be more aware of what is being revealed to your spirit through the Holy Spirit. This is the way to walk with God. It is having your every step guided by the Holy Spirit through your human spirit. The Holy Spirit knows exactly where God is going, and He will get you there.

92 KNOW HIM BY REVELATION

"I want you to know, brothers and sisters, that the gospel I preached is not of human origin. I did not receive it from any man, nor was I taught it; rather, I received it by revelation from Jesus Christ. For you have heard of my previous way of life in Judaism, how intensely I persecuted the church of God and tried to destroy it. I was advancing in Judaism beyond many of my own age among my people and was extremely zealous for the traditions of my fathers. But when God, who set me apart from my mother's womb and called me by His grace, was pleased to reveal His Son in me so that I might preach Him among the Gentiles, my immediate response was not to consult any human being."

– Galatians 1:11-16 (NIV)

Getting to know Jesus through His Word is the most secure way to know Him. Getting to know Him by experience as the best teacher gives you intimacy. Getting to know Him through your spirit as it intertwines with the Holy Spirit is the deepest way to know Him. Yet, the original way to know Him was through revelation. The Bible talks about our spiritual eyes being opened. It talks about people living in darkness and then coming to the light. None of us was able to really see Jesus until God, by His grace, opened our eyes, meaning our ability to perceive, and revealed His Son to us.

This was the case with Saul who was later renamed Paul. Saul had all the education, all the scriptures, and all the Jewish traditions that pointed to the Messiah. Jesus fulfilled every prophecy that was spoken about Him, but Saul just didn't see it until God extended His grace and opened Saul's spiritual sight as He temporarily took his physical sight. Jesus revealed Himself to Saul and kept on giving Saul revelation about Himself. Saul became the Apostle Paul and the revelation he received from Jesus through the Holy Spirit is still speaking to us today through the written word.

In your time with God today, ask Him to reveal more of Himself to you. You really want to know Him. You want intimacy with Him. You want to know Him as a Friend, and a Father … as a Helper, and a Healer … as an Advisor, and an Advocate … as a Guide and a Grantor. There is so much to learn about God, His Son Jesus Christ, and the Holy Spirit. All of them are one God, but there is so much detail in each of them. God is overwhelmingly deep, but we can know Him as He reveals Himself. It's so exciting! And God is excited too! He wants to open your eyes and let you see Who He is and Who He wants to be in you.

93 WALK HUMBLY WITH GOD

"Good and upright is the LORD; therefore, He instructs sinners in His ways. He guides the humble in what is right and teaches them His way."

– Psalm 25:8-9 (NIV)

Almost everything that gets in the way of our walk with God can be traced back to pride and rebellion. Walking with God requires daily obedience and staying in step with Him. It requires giving up our way for His way, our will for His will, and our thoughts for His thoughts. The more we do that, the more closely and effectively we walk with Him. But when we want our way, our will, and our thoughts, we pull away from Him. Not conforming is rebellion, and thinking our way is better, is pride. Not wanting to be embarrassed, or placed outside of our comfort zones, is pride. Not wanting to be put in any position that requires us to concede our rights, is rebellion and pride. We are to walk humbly with God.

The Psalmist says that God will guide the humble in what is right and that He teaches them His ways. It's hard to guide the prideful. The prideful are full of arguments about why it can't be done or why they don't want to do it. The prideful have opinions that they hold as equal to God's. The prideful have to be coaxed and convinced before they concede. The rebellious argue for argument's sake. They don't like the feeling of being controlled by another and they get a thrill out of pushing back. It feels powerful and power is seductive. But the humble understand that they don't know what's best. They have an ability to concede the argument. They can trust that God knows best and so they easily comply with instruction. They are eager to learn. They value God's opinions over their own. They are not fooled into thinking they are self-sufficient. They are not weak by any means. They are just wise and disciplined enough to conform to a higher will.

If you want to truly enjoy a long and loving walk with God, you must do it in humility. As you spend time with Him today, ask Him to show you the areas of your life where you are prideful or rebellious. It may be as subtle as not keeping your prayer time, cheating on your diet, or spending what you should have saved. Or it can be as blatant as committing a crime, engaging in adultery, or lying to a client for personal gain. Whatever the infraction, humble yourself today. Let God instruct you in what is right and make the decision to follow Him without argument, without resistance, and in humble submission to His will for your life. Walk humbly with God.

Naida M. Parson, Ph.D

94 NO ENTITLEMENT

""Suppose one of you has a servant plowing or looking after the sheep. Will he say to the servant when he comes in from the field, 'Come along now and sit down to eat'? Won't he rather say, 'Prepare my supper, get yourself ready and wait on me while I eat and drink; after that you may eat and drink'? Will he thank the servant because he did what he was told to do? So, you also, when you have done everything you were told to do, should say, 'We are unworthy servants; we have only done our duty.'""

– Luke 17:7-10 (NIV)

Affluent societies tend to breed entitled people. People, especially children, who are entitled believe there are some things that the world owes them. They are frustrated when no one wants to help them, or when they are required to expend energy on things for themselves. Their parents become mere providers, and they become consumers, without having to bring anything to the table themselves. They are taught that there are some things they should have for no other reason except they were born into the world. And from what they can see, the world has plenty and they should get their share. But, in our walk with God, there is no room for entitlement. Everything God gives us, including the privilege of being invited to walk with Him, is because of His grace and mercy. Mercy is when He didn't give you the punishment you DID deserve. Grace is when He did give you the blessing you DIDN'T deserve.

In this lesson, Jesus is teaching His disciples the proper attitude we need to walk with Him. When a servant served a master in those days, it was often because they were paying back a debt. The debt might have been financial, or it may have been because their country was defeated and, instead of killing them, they offered them life. Their debt then, was for their very life. In these cases, the proper attitude of a servant was to be grateful for the opportunity to serve and not to feel entitled to anything more, not even a thank you from the master. If you're from an affluent society, or if you're angry at your disenfranchisement, you may have had an indignant reaction to that last statement. You believe all human beings are created equal and are entitled to certain rights. But don't miss the point. God Almighty is not your equal. He has everything. You have nothing. You can't even provide for yourself the air you breathe. Your attitude in your walk with God should be one of no entitlement at all. God owed you nothing but death for your sins, which is total separation from Him. But He chooses to give you the opportunity to walk with Him daily.

No entitlement. In your prayer time today, check your attitude and your motives. Do you get angry with God when things don't go your way? Is there bitterness in your heart when others are blessed with what you have been denied? Do you ever find yourself saying things like "how could this happen to me?" Do you ever think that you should be in a better position because you serve God better, or live better, than others? Then you may have some secret entitlement. The goal is to walk humbly with God, not arrogantly expecting royal treatment. Now God did promise to bless us and provide all we need, and then some. It is perfectly biblical to expect Him to do just that. But never forget it's grace and not what you have earned, so that when He chooses another road for you, you aren't bitter or resentful. He doesn't owe you. He just loves you.

Naida M. Parson, Ph.D

95 IT SPEAKS TO MOTIVE

"Who is wise and understanding among you? Let them show it by their good life, by deeds done in the humility that comes from wisdom. But if you harbor bitter envy and selfish ambition in your hearts, do not boast about it or deny the truth. Such "wisdom" does not come down from heaven but is earthly, unspiritual, demonic. For where you have envy and selfish ambition, there you find disorder and every evil practice."

– James 3:13-16 (NIV)

Have you ever heard the phrase "it's not about you?" Well in your walk with God, as you approach Him daily, and as you speak to Him in prayer, it's not about you. It's never been about you. It's never going to be about you. Don't get me wrong. God is VERY into you. Enough to give His Son Jesus Christ for you. But in return for such mercy and grace, He wants you to not be so into you. We spend way too much time concerned about ourselves. We worry about who likes us, what we are afraid of, or how we are going to make it. We worry about how we appear to others, how we feel, who we are, and what we have to do. We assess how much have we accomplished and wonder if it is ever enough. We can be so self-absorbed, so self-centered, that we miss what's really important in the world and in our walk with God.

In this scripture, James speaks to those who would have true wisdom and understanding. He warns against selfish ambition. Selfish ambition speaks to things you want in life that only benefit you. There is nothing wrong with wanting to be successful and live well. There is nothing wrong with wanting a home, or wanting your book to sell, or for your business to flourish. The question is, why? It speaks to motive. If at any level it's because you want to look good to other people, fit in, feel worthy, or even confirm you're better than others, your motive is wrong. Everything you do should be a "deed done in humility". No selfishness. No self-centeredness.

Today as you walk with God, ask Him to purify your motives. In everything you do, at home, at work, or in the community, make sure your deeds are done with bringing God glory in mind. Understand that everything you have is because God gave it. Understand that without Him you would be nothing. Know that every day is a grace of God, and you live to bring Him glory. When you do well, it is a testimony of how great your God is and how wonderful it is to live for Him and walk with Him. It speaks to motive. No bitterness or selfish ambition allowed. Let every deed be done in humility. Let all glory be to God.

96 THE RIGHT WAY TO LIVE

"You, God, prescribed the right way to live; now You expect us to live it. Oh, that my steps might be steady, keeping to the course You set; Then I'd never have any regrets in comparing my life with Your counsel."

– Psalm 119:4-6 (MESSAGE)

Some people have learned the hard way that the only person they can depend on is themselves. They have been hurt, let down, taken advantage of, and/or abandoned. So, they don't trust, or lean on, anyone except themselves. You may be one of those people. It is a tiring way to be, but it seems safer and more effective. Unfortunately, when you're in intimate relationship with God, this is a lesson you must unlearn. There is no self-sufficiency in our walk with God. Self-sufficiency is a myth anyway. The truth is, we control almost nothing in life. We don't even control whether we wake up in the morning or are able to take our next breath. As you read this, you don't even know what the rest of this day will hold. What God wants is for us to acknowledge that fact, stop our quest for self-sufficiency, and turn to Him for our every move.

This psalm lets us know that the right way to live is all God prescribed. He has an expectation that we will walk the path He set out for us. His paths will make our steps steady. This may be a bold statement, but I believe that if you walk with God, follow His commands, both in His Word and in the leadings of His Spirit, you can get through life without making any devastating mistakes. I mean the kind of mistakes that drastically alter your life for the worse, or that send you down a destructive road. The Psalmist believes that too. "I'd never have any regrets in comparing my life to Your counsel."

So today, realize more and more that you are totally and joyfully dependent on the God that loves you and has your best interest at heart. Ask Him what He would like from you today. Ask Him who you should reach out to, or who to do a favor for. Ask Him about your career, or job, or parenting, or marriage. Lift up to Him your finances and every decision. He is concerned about the things you are concerned about. He is concerned about you. And He is so very able to sustain your life. He alone is sufficient.

Naida M. Parson, Ph.D

97 HONOR WHO GOD IS

"Ascribe to the LORD, you heavenly beings, ascribe to the LORD glory and strength. Ascribe to the LORD the glory due His name; worship the LORD in the splendor of His holiness."

– Psalm 29:1-2 (NIV)

When you venture to walk with One Who is matchless, holy, full of wonders and miraculous power, you must realize how far above you He is. You must honor the incomprehensible fact that the God of the universe wants to take a walk through life with you. We are not to take for granted this awe-inspiring fact. Just because He is the One who came after you, and has made bloody sacrificial provisions just to be with you, that doesn't mean that you get to mentally or spiritually diminish who He is. It's like He is saying, if you're going to be in relationship with Me, you must honor Who I Am.

The closest thing we can relate to this is our relationship with our parents. If we plan on keeping our intimacy with them, we must never forget who they are to us. We don't get to be disrespectful and too common. When we cross that line, they quickly pull us back and remind us who the parents are. Part of being with them is honoring who they are. The same could be said about a president or leader of a country. They may have friends and family, but for the relationship to continue, they can never forget that he or she still holds that high office and all the authority and respect that goes with it.

The Psalmist encourages us to give to God all the glory that is due His name. Ascribe it to Him. Put the honor where it is supposed to be. He is an amazing God. There is no other entity that exists that is sovereign, omniscient, omnipotent, and omnipresent. There is an honor due Him. Walk with Him today in humility and obedience. Ponder in your mind how great He is. Get out into creation, or find pictures of His mountains, and oceans, and sun, and stars, and trees, and flowers. He deserves the honor, glory, and praise. He deserves you. Today as you become more aware of His greatness, give Him you all over again. Honor who He is.

98 AT YOUR BEST OR YOUR WORST ... COME

"Husbands, love your wives, just as Christ loved the church and gave Himself up for her to make her holy, cleansing her by the washing with water through the word, and to present her to Himself as a radiant church, without stain or wrinkle or any other blemish, but holy and blameless."

– Ephesians 5:25-27 (NIV)

Our relationship with Christ is often difficult for us to imagine. The Bible gives many earthly analogies to help us understand how to walk with our God daily. It talks about it as the relationship between parents and children. It speaks of it as the relationship between servant and master, and even friend to friend. God wants us to walk intimately with Him. Yet, there is a deep intimacy in our relationship with God that most religious Christians never pursue. The Bible says the relationship between Christ and His church is like the marriage relationship. The husband's love for his wife is modeled after Christ's love for the church.

In the marriage relationship, the woman and her husband are so intimate that he can see her at her worst and care for her and she is comfortable with it. During childbirth, or sickness, or grief, the woman can be bare in front of her husband and be comforted by him. She can be naked and not ashamed. She can be physically intimate with him and not embarrassed about her body, or her imperfections. She can be open to him emotionally, spiritually, mentally, and physically and never be rejected, or even anxious about it when she knows she is loved for who she is and all she is. When she is at her worst, he can see her at her worst. But when she is doing fine, she honors him enough not to be at her worst in his presence. She will clean up, dress up, fix it up, and perk up in his presence, and especially when she is with him in the presence of others. She makes sure that she honors him by presenting herself and her home in the best light when she knows he will be present. Yet, according to this scripture, she is intimate enough with him that when she just can't get it together, she can allow him to help her clean herself up so he can present her to himself.

So, in our walk with God, we know we can come to Him at our worst. We can come to Him broken, and hurting, and naked, and raw. He will love us, support us, heal us, and comfort us. But we also

Naida M. Parson, Ph.D

honor Him by being at our best when we are not broken. We honor Him by giving Him the best part of our day when we are fresh and not distracted. We honor Him by presenting ourselves to Him with authentic praise and worship, and not the afterthought "thank yous" and cliche' praises. We honor Him when we give our best service to Him and do His work in excellence, and not just give Him the leftovers of our day. Honor God today with some quality time. Serve Him today in a more excellent way. But, if you're having a bad day, come to Him as you are without fear of rejection. He will wash and clean you up Himself, and then present you to Himself. This is the most intimate relationship you should have.

99 YOUR BEST IS BETTER

"Do your best to present yourself to God as one approved, a worker who does not need to be ashamed and who correctly handles the word of truth."

– 2 Timothy 2:15 (NIV)

I want to be at my best for God. It's not that He would love me any more if I'm always at my best. It's not that He would love me less if I come to Him each day lazily and unkempt. I want to be at my best for Him because He deserves that. I honor Him by how I present myself. One marriage tradition prompted the phrase "a bride adorned for her husband." Women were to prepare themselves to be the most beautiful they have ever been on their wedding day. If they were to marry a king, this preparation might go on for a year with treatments for skin, hair, and body. Even now most brides get an elaborate dress and do things with their hair, make up, fingernails, and diet that they may never do again. The man is not allowed to see them until they are prepared. They want that first look to be breathtaking, and often when that happens, the man is brought to tears. Most cultures seem to have some type of tradition for brides to be presented to their new husbands at their best. And the husband, of course, has his best self there as well.

However, after the big day, both seem to relax their standards. Often couples don't honor each other this way after the honeymoon wears off. But there are those who still realize that how you present yourself honors the person you're presenting yourself to. Those individuals make the effort to still be at their best as often as possible. They keep themselves in shape. They "shower, shampoo, and shine." They look nice when they go out, but most of all, they have the right attitude of kindness and attentiveness when their spouse is around. They want to honor the one they love by often presenting themselves at their best. Paul writes to his mentee, Timothy, that he is to do his best to present himself to God in a way that merits approval. For Timothy, that meant being the best minister he could be. He needed to study the word, make sure he interpreted it correctly, and not embarrass his teacher! Many families drill into their children, "don't embarrass the family." That means that there is an expectation of presenting themselves at their best because it reflects on the entire family. So, we do our best to present ourselves to God, both because it honors Him, and because it represents Him.

Naida M. Parson, Ph.D

When you spend time with God today, don't just give Him your left-over time. Don't just present Him with your tired self, your distracted self, your preoccupied self, your worried self, or your lazy self. He loves all of you and will accept all of you, but can He have the best of you, sometimes? Can you present Him with an excellent praise, sometimes? Can you do an excellent job at whatever ministry you offer Him? Can you come to Him and spend time with Him when you are rested, and alert, and excited to be with Him? This week examine how you present yourself to God and honor Him by being at your best as you walk with Him … mind, body, and spirit. He'll like that.

100 NEVER FORGET WHO GOD IS

"When I consider Your heavens, the work of Your fingers, the moon, and the stars, which You have set in place, what is mankind that You are mindful of them, human beings that You care for them? You have made them a little lower than the angels and crowned them with glory and honor."

— Psalm 8:3-5 (NIV)

In walking with God, there is one lesson we all tend to learn the hard way: We are not equals. No matter how intimate we get with Him and how much of an everyday part He becomes in our lives, we must realize Who we are in relationship with for this relationship to work. You are walking with the Sovereign God. He is your Father. He is your friend. He is your confidant. But He is not your equal. You will never have an equal say, or vote, in this relationship. He is never wrong, and He has veto authority. He won't always use it. Most times He will give you what you choose. But the minute you override His authority and go your own way, you are no longer walking with Him. Walking with God means recognizing that He is your God, your Master, your Lord.

David had an extremely close love relationship with God, yet he is the writer who could not phantom God's willingness to be in relationship with mankind. Considering the vast greatness of God, David asked the question, what is man that you are mindful of him? What are human beings that you care about them so deeply? Mankind is not even the highest created being. Humans were created lower than the angels. We are fickle and inferior, yet we have been given dominion of the earth and the glory of God rests on us. It is an honor to walk with God. It is an honor to be able to have an audience with Him daily in prayer. It is a privilege to have the freedom to ask Him questions, carry His words, and be involved in His mission for this world.

Today, honor the fact that you are in relationship with God Almighty. He is not your equal partner. You are to worship and obey Him. You are to live in submission to His will. You are to be respectful and honor His presence. You are to love Him with all your heart, soul, mind, and strength. You are to trade your thoughts for His thoughts, and your ways for His ways. And you do it joyfully and thankfully. Because, despite His superiority, He wants you to share with Him what you think, and feel, and want to do with your life. He wants you to feel a safe intimacy with Him. He really wants this relationship to work. Walking with Him means that He is taking you somewhere, and He wants to get you there more than you want to go. So, enjoy a good talk with Him today. Just never forget Who you're talking to.

Naida M. Parson, Ph.D

101 HUMBLE YOURSELF

"Humble yourselves, therefore, under God's mighty hand, that He may lift you up in due time."

— 1 Peter 5:6 (NIV)

Submission. Humility. Surrender. These are not words that fare well in our society. At least not in "western civilization." Perhaps religious circles are the only place these words have value anymore. Why is that? Why does mankind have such a difficult time with submission? Perhaps it's because we were created to have dominion. God placed leadership in all of us. We were created for the purpose of having dominion over all the earth. Ever notice that when the woman received her consequences for sinning in the Garden of Eden, one of the things she lost was the right to rule herself in the marriage relationship? She wasn't supposed to like it. It was a curse. She was created to have dominion just like Adam! Submission doesn't come easy for us, even when we are in relationship with a Superior Being. Part of the temptation we fell for was the pride of life. Satan told us we could be like God, and we went for it. It's the same thing Satan went for and got kicked out of the heaven.

So, humility and submission must be taught and practiced. Peter is one who should know. He was a man's man. Dominant, and powerful, and a born leader. Yet, he writes to us that we are to humble ourselves under God's mighty hand and let God lift us up when He decides we are ready. Humble YOURSELF under God's mighty hand. You must do this yourself. It is God's will that we recognize His hand is mighty above any other power on earth and we bring ourselves under it. Peter found out tragically that God is always right. His pride brought him some of the toughest days of his life. But his humility under God's hand made him one of the greatest and most powerful Christian leaders to have ever lived.

God wants to lift you up to heights of effectiveness that you can't imagine. He wants your life to work. He wants to use you to expand His Kingdom. He wants to make you a blessing to others and give you a wonderful and fulfilling life. But it starts with your humility, and submission, and surrender to His will for you. As you walk with Him today, ask Him again how you can please Him. What does He want from you today? How can you serve Him today? And if it's something you don't want to do, then humbly submit yourself and do it anyway. This must become your way of life. When you get this part of walking with God into a consistent lifestyle, you will find yourself lifted in ways that will blow your mind!

102 HE'S GOD ... AND THAT'S JUST THE WAY IT IS

"I Am the Lord, and there is no other; apart from Me there is no God. I will strengthen you, though you have not acknowledged Me, so that from the rising of the sun to the place of its setting people may know there is none besides Me. I Am the Lord, and there is no other. I form the light and create darkness, I bring prosperity and create disaster; I, the Lord, do all these things. "You heavens above, rain down My righteousness; let the clouds shower it down. Let the earth open wide, let salvation spring up, let righteousness flourish with it; I, the Lord, have created it."

– Isaiah 45:5-8 (NIV)

We are in relationship with the God of the universe! Some religions make Him too much like them, especially when it comes to Jesus. Of Him, they often say, He is a man like many other great men who were also sons of God. They consider Him great, but not divine. As far as God is concerned, they liken Him to nature, saying God is all around us, or that there is God in all of us. Some say He is just a concept like a good force in the universe and the opposite of evil. Mankind tends to create God in his, or her, own image instead of the other way around. But God is God. He is the Sovereign, all knowing, all-powerful, ever-present Creator of the world, and if we are going to walk with Him, we must be always aware of Who He is.

He identifies Himself so powerfully to the prophet Isaiah. "I Am the Lord, and there is no other; apart from Me there is no God." There were many who questioned God and His decisions. There were some corrective things He needed to do with His people that they may not have liked or understood. So, He reminds them of Who they are dealing with! He is their Lord, meaning He is the One with control and authority. There is no other God apart from Him. Though they were in a world that acknowledged idol gods, He is the only true God that exists. And though they didn't always acknowledge Him, He was still their God. They would soon know that there is no other God, but Him. He is the Creator of light and darkness. He has the power to bring them good or allow them to suffer. He will always prove to be right no matter what!

Naida M. Parson, Ph.D

As you walk with God again today, acknowledge Him, worship Him, and exalt Him for Who He is. Let Him know that despite your complaints, and questions, and open conversation that He allows you to freely have with Him, you recognize that He is your Lord. You recognize He is the Creator, and you consider it a privilege to be able to talk with Him as a Father and friend. Let Him know, and perhaps remind yourself, that what He says goes and when it is all said, it's His will that must be done. He is God, and that's just the way it is.

103 YOUR ARM'S TOO SHORT TO BOX WITH GOD

"Woe to those who quarrel with their Maker, those who are nothing but potsherds among the potsherds on the ground. Does the clay say to the potter, 'What are you making?' Does your work say, 'The potter has no hands'? Woe to the one who says to a father, 'What have you begotten?' or to a mother, 'What have you brought to birth?' "This is what the Lord says— the Holy One of Israel, and its Maker: Concerning things to come, do you question Me about My children, or give Me orders about the work of My hands? It is I who made the earth and created mankind on it. My own hands stretched out the heavens; I marshaled their starry hosts."

– Isaiah 45:9-12 (NIV)

Our relationship with God is, for sure, a complete relationship like all of our others. We disagree with each other. We get angry with each other. We have times we decline to talk to each other. We make up, and come to agreement, and move on. We laugh and cry together, and experience life. But, on the other hand, it's like no other relationship we will ever have because there are some things about God that are like no one else. He is always right. He will never lose the argument. You can voice your opinion respectfully, but knowing that you could never get Him to understand anything different than what He already knows. I saw a play once entitled "Your Arm's Too Short To Box With God!" No matter what, God will prevail.

As God continues to declare Himself through Isaiah, you would think that He is insulted by the questioning of His judgment. The scripture does not forbid us to ask God questions. It simply points out that our wisdom and our will can never supersede His. We can ask Him to give us understanding, but woe to us if we quarrel with Him to the point of rebellion over His plans and purposes for the world He created, and for the human beings He made. Woe to us, especially if we think we can give Him orders. In this relationship you will always be subordinate. So, your response should always be submission rather than argument.

Today as you walk and talk with God, feel free to ask Him anything you wish. If there are things you have been wondering about, even about your own life, He is waiting to have that conversation

Naida M. Parson, Ph.D

with you. Just know that He is your Maker. He is the One who stretched out the heavens with His own hands. He knows what He is doing and why He allowed what He allows. And He knows what He is doing with you. Since you can't box with Him, you may as well trust Him. He is a potter Who knows exactly what He is making and how it should be made. You are a work of art! Stop fighting and quarreling with Him. You will love the final result.

104 WE LIVE FOR THE LORD

"For none of us lives for ourselves alone, and none of us dies for ourselves alone. If we live, we live for the Lord; and if we die, we die for the Lord. So, whether we live or die, we belong to the Lord."

– Romans 14:7-8 (NIV)

Include God in everything you do, no matter how mundane or human it seems to be. Know that every day you live, you live at His discretion. He wants to enjoy those days with you, and He wants to help you make the best of them. He is interested in everything that concerns you. Everything. I'm not saying that you should ask Him what color underwear to put on, or if you should have seafood or chicken for dinner. But how you eat and what you wear are His concern, and if there is a reason to ask Him, He will lead and guide and share.

This scripture is from Paul who was explaining how Jews and Gentiles could live peacefully together even though they had different traditions. In the middle of his argument, he makes this observation. We don't live for ourselves anymore. We live for the Lord. He is our life now. Everything is for Him. How we live our everyday lives is directly related to our relationship with Him. You should seek to know how He feels about your wardrobe, your diet, your presentation, your job choice, your financial habits, your other relationships, and your plans. Where does He need you to be? What mission does He have for you today? We live for the Lord.

Make the effort today to include Him more and more in the everyday things you do. Thank Him for your meals. Acknowledge Him in what you wear. Consult Him about money matters. Pray about your children and spouse and how your household should be structured for maximum positive effect. Examine your life and see if there is an area where you have left God out. If there is, invite Him in. It just might be life changing.

Naida M. Parson, Ph.D

105 DON'T MAKE A MOVE WITHOUT GOD

"When David and his men reached Ziklag, they found it destroyed by fire and their wives and sons and daughters taken captive. So, David and his men wept aloud until they had no strength left to weep. David's two wives had been captured—Ahinoam of Jezreel and Abigail, the widow of Nabal of Carmel. David was greatly distressed because the men were talking of stoning him; each one was bitter in spirit because of his sons and daughters. But David found strength in the Lord his God. Then David said to Abiathar the priest, the son of Ahimelek, "Bring me the ephod." Abiathar brought it to him, and David inquired of the Lord, "Shall I pursue this raiding party? Will I overtake them?" "Pursue them," He answered. "You will certainly overtake them and succeed in the rescue.""

— 1 Samuel 30:3-8 (NIV)

People who walk closely with God have a tendency to ask Him about everything and include Him in everything. The wisdom of the Book of Proverbs states that we should acknowledge Him in all our ways. It suggests that leaning to our understanding of life is not the wisest action. Maybe the intention was not an extreme ALL, but it did say "all." I suppose that no matter what the original Hebrew word is, "all" meant "all." David may not have asked God everything at every time, but as a man who walked with God, He was sure to include Him even in things that may have been what we would consider a "no brainer."

David was a warrior. War is what he did for a living. War was what he was anointed to do. It was the call on his life. And he was in a season of war with an army God provided for him. So, when his own town was attacked and his wives and children were taken captive, you would think that this was a "no brainer" for sure. Yet, when his men turned on him and his leadership was questioned, David went to the One he walked with. He went to the One Person whose support he could not do without. He wanted to know from God if this was the right time to do what he was created to do. He had just come from a battle he wasn't supposed to fight. Then horrible things happened while he was gone and something worse was about to happen if he didn't move quickly. But not so fast this time. David had to check in with God and he didn't move until he got an answer. He didn't move until he knew God was with him.

What do you need to move on today? What situations and circumstances are pressing you into action? What are the things you are born to do that you go about doing without even thinking for the most part? Take time to pray about those things today. Don't make a move without knowing He is with you, even if it seems like a "no brainer". Remember, this devotional is about walking "with" God, not out in front of Him, lagging behind Him, or on another street altogether. There may be some "no brainers" in life, but when you're walking with God there is never a "no prayer."

Naida M. Parson, Ph.D

106 MAKE DECISIONS TOGETHER

"Ahab king of Israel asked Jehoshaphat king of Judah, "Will you go with me against Ramoth Gilead?" Jehoshaphat replied, "I am as you are, and my people as your people; we will join you in the war." But Jehoshaphat also said to the king of Israel, "First seek the counsel of the Lord.""

— 2 Chronicles 18:3-4 (NIV)

When you walk with God there should be no major decision that is not a decision you and God make together. In a marriage, once you take on a spouse, your lives are now one life. You no longer have the right to go rogue and make major decisions that will affect the entire family on your own. Hopefully, your family has some goals and a vision for where you are going as a team. Any decision you make effects the team, so when it's time to choose a direction, the family gets together to talk about it and choose a plan of action. This is especially true when you aren't the team lead.

Jehoshaphat, King of Judah understood this more than Ahab, King of Israel. Ahab wanted to go to war and asked Jehoshaphat to go with him since they were all Hebrews. The difference between them was that Jehoshaphat walked with God. Before he would make a decision that would put their lives in danger, put the family of God at risk, and perhaps change their status in the region, he wanted to find out what God had to say about it. He asked for counsel from the Lord. He understood that God had a purpose and plan for their lives, that God was the team lead, not Ahab. Jehoshaphat didn't want to go forward without a word from the Lord.

God has a purpose and plan for your life, too. He knows where He is taking you and has planned out your every step. But you are a free willed being. You can make decisions on your own. Walking with God means giving up that right and submitting to a will higher than your own. It's trusting your team lead and understanding that God always has your best interest at heart. And, as my mother used to say to me, "He can see way down the road." So today, put this priceless principle in your way of life as a person who walks with God. Every life decision you make is a decision you and God have made together. He will always listen to your wants, needs, and heart desires, and He will always weigh them against His plans and purposes for your life. He will get you where you really want to be, and more importantly, where you need to be.

*Devotions 107 - 139 are influenced by the book, The Five Love Languages by Gary Chapman. Mr. Chapman asserts that people give and receive love differently and describes them as five languages: Words of Affirmation, Quality Time, Acts of Service, Gift Giving, and Physical Touch.

107 LIVE IN LOVE

"And so, we know and rely on the love God has for us. God is love. Whoever lives in love lives in God, and God in them."

— 1 John 4:16 (NIV)

What a beautiful verse of scripture spoken by the beloved disciple and friend of Jesus, the Apostle John. "Whoever lives in love … ". If you have ever truly been in love, this scripture takes on a deeper meaning. How glorious it is to live in love, to be able stay in that place, to be passionate about our Savior every day, and subsequently share that love with others. It is God's will that we live in love.

God is love. This means more than God loves. It means that love is the very essence of who God is. There is a book by Gary Chapman that talks about five love languages. They are Words of Affirmation, Quality Time, Acts of Service, Gift Giving, and Physical Touch. Because God is love, I believe He speaks all five fluently! In developing more and more intimacy with Him, we can offer Him all five love languages and receive all five from Him. God is love. He is a lover. He is relational. All He ever wanted from us is to be in love relationship with Him. Everything else flows from that. He speaks all five love languages fluently and so should you.

Every day, offer God some words of affirmation in the form of praise. Every day, spend some quality time with Him. Every day, ask Him what acts of service you can do for Him and what gifts you can offer to Him, or someone else on behalf of Him. Every day, touch Him in some way through your spirit man. And, let Him do the same for you. Love goes both ways. He wants time with you. He wants to touch your life. He wants to give you good gifts and do acts of service for you. He wants to tell you who you are to Him and affirm you. Live in love. Stay there. Abide there. God is love and to walk with Him means to experience it in the most amazing ways.

108 HEART, SOUL, MIND, AND STRENGTH

"One of the teachers of the law came and heard them debating. Noticing that Jesus had given them a good answer, he asked Him, "Of all the commandments, which is the most important?" "The most important one," answered Jesus, "is this: 'Hear, O Israel: The Lord our God, the Lord is One. Love the Lord your God with all your heart and with all your soul and with all your mind and with all your strength.'"

– Mark 12:28-30 (NIV)

Of all the things the Holy Scriptures instruct us to do, to feel, and to be, Jesus declares that there is one that is most important: Love the Lord your God with all your heart, soul, mind, and strength. God is love and we were created to be in love relationship with Him. It is our major purpose. It is His greatest desire. It is what makes Him smile. Loving God serves as the basis of everything else we do in life. It is our reason. It is our "why" when everything else fades away.

Jesus was not hesitant to answer the question as to what the greatest commandment was. He goes to the book of Deuteronomy and pulls out this original command. Love God. In essence, love Me. But, more than that, love God with ALL your heart, soul, mind, and strength. Your heart is the innermost part of who you are and includes your spirit. Your soul is the seat of your emotions. Your mind is your thought life. Your strength is from your physical body. There is much debate about the difference between soul, mind, spirit, and heart as to what means what. But the point is that this is a total being love. It is emotional, mental, spiritual, and physical. It involves the will, the thoughts, the actions, and the motives. Everything in you, and everything about you, should be governed by the overriding fact that you love God.

Today, love Him with your words. Tell Him repeatedly how much you love Him. Sing it in a song. Write it in a poem. Put it on a sticky note and post it where you can see it. Show Him with your actions. Do something loving for someone today to love Him through His children. Live in obedience today. Do what is right out of love for Him. Express it passionately. Give Him your emotions. Set your will to live a life in love. And keep reading as we further develop the most important part of this devotional: learning to love the God we are walking with.

Naida M. Parson, Ph.D

109 A TWO-SIDED RELATIONSHIP

"After the king was settled in his palace and the Lord had given him rest from all his enemies around him, he said to Nathan the prophet, "Here I am, living in a house of cedar, while the ark of God remains in a tent." Nathan replied to the king, "Whatever you have in mind, go ahead and do it, for the Lord is with you."

"Go and tell my servant David, 'This is what the Lord says: Are you the one to build Me a house to dwell in?

…. The Lord declares to you that the Lord Himself will establish a house for you:"

— 2 Samuel 7:1-3, 5, 11b (NIV)

In offering the Lord the love languages, remember that this relationship must go both ways. Not only do we offer them to Him, but we must receive the expression of love from Him. If we offer Him an act of service, we must also receive acts of service from Him. If we offer Him words of affirmation about Who He is to us, we will also hear words from Him about who we are to Him. If we give Him a gift, we can also receive gifts from Him. If He gives us His quality time, we in turn, should make sure we spend quality time with Him. When we feel His touch on our lives, we should reach out to touch Him back. Of course, because He is God and exists in the spirit realm, this may be a creative challenge. But the whole point of us being created is to walk with God. The expressions of love must go both ways.

David was as relational as can be with God. Perhaps this is how he earned the title of being a man after God's own heart. David received abundance from God, but his love for God made him want to do the same for Him. How could he live in a great palace and keep the presence of God, the Ark of the Covenant, in a tent? It was David's desire to honor God as God had honored him. Then God says to him, "you want to build Me a house? I appreciate that. I never asked for it, but you want to do that for Me? You aren't in a position to do it, but I will allow your son to do it. And, instead of you making Me a house, I'm going to make YOU a house! And it will be more than a material house. It will be a house that will live forever." With Jesus coming through the lineage of David, God has kept His promise.

God and David loved on each other from the time David was writing songs on the side of a mountain. Their love story was never one-sided. Your love story with God won't be one-sided either. As you learn to love on God and offer Him these love languages, also allow Him to love on you and receive the love languages from Him. Start today. There is nothing like being in a vibrant love relationship with God! And there is nothing more precious to Him than to be in this relationship with you.

110 AFFIRMATIVE PRAISE

"I will bless the Lord at all times: His praise shall continually be in my mouth. My soul shall make her boast in the Lord: the humble shall hear thereof, and be glad. O magnify the Lord with me, and let us exalt His name together."

– Psalms 34:1-3 (KJV)

As you begin your walk with God each morning, throughout the day, and even as the last thing at night, offer God some affirmative praise. Chapman calls this love language "words of affirmation." To affirm means to make firm what you believe to be true by agreeing and receiving it and making it part of your own truth. We love people to affirm us by telling us we are loved and/or special in some way. For some people, it doesn't matter what you do for them, or how much time you spend with them, they need to hear you say, "I love you", "you did that so very well", "you're an amazing friend".

God responds to our praise. David understood this and made it a point to praise God regularly. Here in this psalm David declares that he blesses the Lord at all times, and His praise is continually in his mouth. The word bless usually means "to speak well of". David spoke well of the Lord. His soul boasted in the Lord. He bragged on Him. He had great things to say about Him. He affirmed many ways that God was exactly what He claimed to be. Most importantly, God had been these things to him personally. He affirmed what he knew to be true about God.

Affirmative praise is more than boosting the ego of God. God is not insecure and doesn't need to be affirmed for Him to be okay with Himself. Affirmation is a form of loving God. But the by product is for you and God knows that. The more you affirm Who He is, the more you have faith and confidence in His ability to care for you, and the more you can live free from anxiety and fear. The more you affirm Who He is, the more you can go through life knowing that the God of Heaven is able to sustain you in every way. You affirm that He is, and always will be, all you need and everything you ever wanted. Do that today. Tell God Who He is to you. Affirm all that He has been in your life. He loves it. You will too.

111 WHO IS GOD TO YOU?

"The Lord is my shepherd, I lack nothing."

— Psalm 23:1 (NIV)

"The Lord is my light and my salvation— whom shall I fear? The Lord is the stronghold of my life— of whom shall I be afraid?"

— Psalm 27:1 (NIV)

"The Lord is my rock, my fortress and my deliverer; my God is my rock, in whom I take refuge, my shield and the horn of my salvation, my stronghold."

— Psalm 18:2 (NIV)

"Who is God?" is the question religions have struggled with since religion was created. But we are not merely religious. We are in relationship with the Almighty God. We have gone so far beyond wondering if there is a God, and if so, who is He? We are believers. We believe that there is a God. We believe that He is the Creator and that He is Our Father revealed to us through His Son Jesus Christ. So, in walking with God, a better question for us is "Who is God to you?" Affirm to Him who He is to you as you share your affirmative praise today. It is great to talk to God about Who He is in the universe, but to love on Him truly and intimately, it's important to experience and express Who He is to you.

This is what King David, the psalmist, did so proficiently. He constantly affirmed Who God was to him by using everyday things people could relate to. More importantly, he used things that were a part of his personal life to express how he experienced God. David was a shepherd, so he affirms to God that He is his Shepherd and because of that, David has everything he needs. David has been in the dark naturally and has needed a light to see his way. So, when he is in the dark spiritually and needs to see his way, he affirms the Lord is my Light. David is a warrior and has been in a stronghold and a fortress. He has hidden himself in a rock and has stood on a rock to fight. He has held up a shield to protect himself. Yet, he realizes that his true protection came from God, so he affirms, "God, You are my Stronghold, my Fortress, my Rock, and my Shield."

Naida M. Parson, Ph.D

Sometimes to compare God to created or manmade things seems to trivialize Him, but we are finite human beings, and we can't put God into words that match Him. So, we come as close as we can with our affirmative praises. He is my Father and my Friend. He is my Master and my Pastor. He is the lifter of my head and the forgiver of my sin. He is the air I breathe. He is my reason, my why and my what for. He is my constant companion. He is my light when shadows fall. He is an excellent therapist. He has been a husband to me, a great provider, and peace in my storms. He is a sustainer and the center of my joy. Affirm to Him what He is to you today, and as you walk with Him the rest of your life that list will grow longer and deeper as you go.

112 DO YOU TRUST HIM?

"In You, Lord my God, I put my trust. I trust in You; do not let me be put to shame, nor let my enemies triumph over me.

Guide me in Your truth and teach me, for You are God my Savior, and my hope is in You all day long."

— Psalm 25:1-2, 5 (NIV)

Another way to affirm God is to confess your faith in Him. Do you trust Him? Tell Him that. Of course, He already knows how you feel, but in affirming to Him that you trust Him, you actually build that trust up in your relationship. If you haven't figured this out yet, the affirmations of praise to God do more for us than they do for Him. He does love the sound of our praise (remember, God is relational), but when we affirm our trust in Him, it also changes us and affirms in us that we are in good hands.

So again, do you trust Him? It is an act of your will. David writes in this psalm, that he "put" his trust in the Lord. He resolved to place all his trust there in hopes that he will not regret it or be put to shame if it doesn't work out. In a sense he is saying "God I'm placing all bets on You, don't let me lose! Don't embarrass me!" David writes, "my hope is in you all day long." David trusted everything in his day to God and wanted God to know it. We don't always know what God is going to do. We don't know what He is going to allow to happen in our lives. But we have made the decision to put our trust in Him, and hope in Him, all day long.

To trust God means to trust in His love for you, believing that He will do you no harm, even when it seems like He is the one hurting you, because sometimes it will. It means to trust His character, knowing that He is a good and faithful God, even when you don't understand Him, because sometimes you won't. It means to trust His ability to heal it, fix it, change it, and work it out, even if it seems like He isn't going to, because sometimes it will. It means to trust His judgment, believing He will do what is right, even if you don't agree with Him, because sometimes you won't. Affirm your trust in Him today and keep walking … all day long.

Naida M. Parson, Ph.D

113 AFFIRMATION GOES BOTH WAYS

"But the angel said to her, "Do not be afraid, Mary; you have found favor with God."

– Luke 1:30 (NIV)

Can you imagine being a young lady just going about your day, planning your wedding perhaps, or at least wondering what your groom is planning, and preparing yourself for the next season in your life when you get a message from God? The message is basically "I like you and I Am with you." Now that's an affirmation! That the God of heaven, first of all, even sees you! That of all the people in the world, He has noticed you. You. It is to you, seemingly insignificant to the world up until that day, that God affirms, not only that He sees you, but that you have favor with Him. He affirms that He likes you, and most importantly, that He is with you in everything you are about to do. This is where Mary, the mother of Jesus, found herself that day. And because of Jesus, we are in that place every day we walk with God.

As you give Him your affirmative praise-praising Him and affirming to Him Who He is to you-also receive affirmation from Him. Let Him tell you who you are to Him. As you tell Him Who He is, He wants to tell you who you are. All these love languages go both ways. All throughout the scriptures, God has affirmed His chosen men and women, His chosen nation, and of course, His chosen Son. He tells them He loves them. He tells them He has prepared great things for them. He tells them they have been predestined. God loves to affirm His children who walk with Him. He may do it through your prayer if you know His voice. He may do it through a scripture during your reading. He may speak to you through a song, or a sermon. Allow God to affirm you and receive that affirmation from Him.

In case you haven't heard, you are highly favored of God, and He is with you. He likes you. He made you because you were what He wanted to make. He sees you in spite of how insignificant you may feel in this world. He has plans for you that He developed and implemented Himself. You have found favor with Him. He has loved you with an everlasting love. No good thing will He withhold from you. He loves walking with you, and He will be with you until you are eventually with Him in His paradise that He is preparing as we speak. Be affirmed by your Father today. You who are highly favored, don't be afraid. You have found favor with God.

114 JUST SAY AMEN

""I am the Lord's servant," Mary answered. "May your word to me be fulfilled." Then the angel left her.

And Mary said: "My soul glorifies the Lord, and my spirit rejoices in God my Savior, for He has been mindful of the humble state of His servant. From now on all generations will call me blessed, for the Mighty One has done great things for me— holy is His name."

– Luke 1:38, 46-49 (NIV)

When God begins to share words of affirmation with you, agree with what He says about you. Accept the compliment. One thing that women are notoriously known for is not accepting compliments. You can tell a woman her dress is nice, and she will tell you how old it is. If you tell her that hair looks good, she will tell you that she doesn't like the color. If you tell her that her face is pretty, she will tell you all the blemishes she has covered up with makeup. Some of us do it out of false modesty. Some of us do it out of true insecurity. Men sometimes have the better idea. We call it male ego or being braggadocios. But maybe it's simply accepting affirmation. When God speaks of us and tells us who we are in Him, we are to accept what He is saying. Agree with Him. Who could be more right than God?

When Mary heard from the angel that she was to be the mother of Jesus, the Son of God, the Savior of the world, she did have some questions. How could this be? She had some concerns. What kind of greeting is this, telling me I have God's favor? But after everything was explained, she accepted the affirmation. She said, "I am the Lord's servant … May your word to me be fulfilled". She said, "generations will call me blessed." She was not bragging. She was accepting what God said about her. She basically gave God an "Amen". So be it. Truth.

As you and God walk together and love on each other today, use words of affirmation. Come to Him in affirmative praise and tell Him Who He is. Tell Him Who He is to you, personally. And when He loves back on you by affirming you and telling you who you are and who you are to Him, accept what He is saying. He is always going to be right, and He is right about you! Don't throw His words back to Him in denial. It doesn't matter whether you see it right now. Just His word will make it so. Don't give Him an "aww man! That couldn't be me. I don't see that." And don't give Him a "come on man! That couldn't be my call or my destiny." Just give Him an Amen. I am Your servant. May Your word to me be fulfilled. Amen? Amen.

Naida M. Parson, Ph.D

115 GIFT GIVING

"Which of you, if your son asks for bread, will give him a stone? Or if he asks for a fish, will give him a snake? If you, then, though you are evil, know how to give good gifts to your children, how much more will your Father in heaven give good gifts to those who ask Him!"

– Matthew 7:9-11 (NIV)

Gift giving is the love language that is closest to the essence of Who God is. The most beloved verse in the gospel is John 3:16 that says, "for God so loved... He gave." Loving and giving go hand in hand. Love makes you give of yourself and your substance. It motivates you to give your time and your energy. Love makes you put yourself second and the one you love in first place in your life.

Jesus, in describing how the Father feels about us, compares Him to earthly fathers. Parents love their children and provide for them good things. How much more does our Heavenly Father want to give to us good gifts? He is a gift giver. He has blessings in store for His children, and when we ask in prayer as we walk with Him daily, He is not just willing, but He is excited to give good gifts to us. Don't shy away from it. Don't feel unworthy of it. Don't be afraid to ask. It is His love language to give. In the book of Romans, Paul reminds us that He has already given us the best He had. He gave His Son. Why would He withhold anything else?

As you walk and talk with God today, ask Him for the things you need. Ask Him for some things you just desire. Good gifts include the ability to love more, perfect peace, real joy, and godly patience. Good gifts include leadership, musical ability, teaching, or prayer. Good gifts include family, friends, or great business associates. Great gifts are new souls added to the kingdom and a boldness to witness. Just know that gift giving is His language, and He is waiting to communicate with you on this level. What good gift can you think of today?

116 GIVE HIM YOUR GIFTS

"Again, it will be like a man going on a journey, who called his servants and entrusted his wealth to them. To one he gave five bags of gold, to another two bags, and to another one bag, each according to his ability. Then he went on his journey. The man who had received five bags of gold went at once and put his money to work and gained five bags more. So also, the one with two bags of gold gained two more. But the man who had received one bag went off, dug a hole in the ground and hid his master's money."

– Matthew 25:14-18 (NIV)

Walking with God is all about our love relationship with Him. The love goes both ways. In the love language of gift giving, it's more than what God gives to you. It is also about returning those gifts to God. In the Old Testament, King David said that they were giving God only what came from His hand. We realize that every gift we have comes from God, and because we love Him, we are motivated to give back to Him our gifts and talents and substance.

Jesus tells the parable here of three servants who were given gifts from their master. Two of them put their gifts to work and doubled them in value. One of them took his gift and buried it. When the master returned, he was quite angry with the servant who did nothing with what he was given. In loving on God, we should take what He has given us and offer it back to Him. Give Him your gift. Then, whatever you find to do with it, do it excellently and diligently. Improve on it, work on it, learn about it and offer it to the kingdom of God. This includes actual money like in this story. Lovers are givers. Your financial support of God's agenda in this world is in direct relationship with how you love Him. Where you spend your time, your energy, and your money is a great indication of who you love and worship.

What gifts do you have to offer God? As you pray and spend time with Him today, ask Him what gift He wants from you. Ask Him what He would like you to offer up to Him today. You may be a writer and He wants you to write to encourage someone, or work on that book. You may be a singer and He would like you to sing to Him or do some work on that project. You may be great with kids, and He wants to you find some children today to interact with or encourage. You may have a few dollars in the bank, and He wants you to share an extra tip with the waitress or give to a cause that's on His heart. Ask Him what He wants from you as you tell Him what you want from Him. And just like He gives good gifts, give to Him excellently and enthusiastically. God loves a cheerful giver.

Naida M. Parson, Ph.D

117 NO COMPENSATION REQUIRED

"Wealth and honor come from You; You are the Ruler of all things. In Your hands are strength and power to exalt and give strength to all. Now, our God, we give You thanks, and praise Your glorious Name. "But who am I, and who are my people, that we should be able to give as generously as this? Everything comes from You, and we have given You only what comes from Your hand."

— 1 Chronicles 29:12-14 (NIV)

We often give gifts with the unspoken expectation of getting something in return. Sometimes it's as obvious as buying a birthday, or Christmas gift for someone we know will return the favor. Sometimes, it's subtle. We give gifts hoping to be loved, or appreciated, or held on to. We give out of the fear of rejection or abandonment. Sometimes we give for the joy of seeing the person we love fawn over the gift. We at least want them to appreciate it, and even more so, appreciate the giver. Even when it comes to giving to God, we are often motivated by what we expect to receive back from Him. We tithe so we can receive open windows of heaven and blessings we don't have room to receive. We "sow seed offerings" to get the harvest later. The gifts and talents many people give to their church is often done only when there is a paid position. All this giving and receiving is biblical, but as you walk with God, some things you should offer up with no compensation because you are giving your gifts to Him.

This is the kind of giving King David talked about. As they were preparing to give to the temple, David begins to be so excited that he prays and praises. He declares that the ability to give to God is an absolute honor. Who are they to be able to give such small tokens to a great and mighty God? And then he says the truest statement on giving ever stated. We give God only what comes from His hand! We haven't truly given Him anything. Anything we give to God is only given back to Him. He gives us gifts, and talents, and wealth, and health, and the breath that we breathe. He gives us the activity of our bodies and the power to gain and accumulate increase. If we give Him our gift of song, it's because He gave us voice. If we give Him our gift of writing, it's because He originates the words. If we give Him a monetary offering, it's because He provided. So why would we only give to get even more from Him?

Offer God your gifts and talents daily. Ask Him in prayer what He would like you to do with your gifts that day. Ask Him what you can offer Him. And when you do, do it without expectation of compensation. Musicians, singers, pastors, administrators, and even church secretaries should have the attitude that they would serve God with their gifts whether they were being paid or not. And if you don't fit any of those categories, when you give an offering to God, you don't always need a tax letter, or a record kept. He may want you to give to someone and no one will ever know. But what an honor to be able to give to God Himself! That makes it a genuine love language. The only motivation is "I love you" and "I'm grateful". Lovers are givers. And, by the way, when you give like that, of yourself, your gifts, or your wealth, with no expectation of compensation or blessing, He will always give back to you, anyway. He is a lover. Lovers are givers.

Naida M. Parson, Ph.D

118   GOD WON'T FORGET A GIVER

"At Caesarea there was a man named Cornelius, a centurion in what was known as the Italian Regiment. He and all his family were devout and God-fearing; he gave generously to those in need and prayed to God regularly. One day at about three in the afternoon he had a vision. He distinctly saw an angel of God, who came to him and said, "Cornelius!" Cornelius stared at him in fear. "What is it, Lord?" he asked. The angel answered, "Your prayers and gifts to the poor have come up as a memorial offering before God."

— Acts 10:1-4 (NIV)

Gift giving to God can come in many forms. It includes finances, time, and energy. Your whole existence is a gift from God, so your whole existence can be a gift to God. When we think of offering God our gifts, we often think of talent and abilities. Secondarily, we think of offerings given at a church, or through a church. These are certainly the things we want to offer God on a daily and weekly basis. It is part of our worship. But God has also given us energy and stamina. He has given us the precious gift of time. And of course, our financial blessings and resources including our homes, cars, and food.

Cornelius was a good devout man who had a giving heart. This scripture doesn't speak of his religion, or if he was part of a temple where he could give offerings. We just see that he gave to the poor and that he gave God time in prayer. God remembered every coin he gave to the poor, for as Jesus said, whatever we do for the least, we do for Him. God remembered all the time and energy he spent. Because of this, he was chosen to be the first Gentile to receive Christ. His giving of time, energy, and finance outside of the normal religious venues, granted him favor with God.

Today, find someone to give to just for the joy of giving. You may be the answer to someone's prayer today. Expend some energy by going out of your way to shop for someone, clean up a yard, give a parent a break, or teach someone to read. Dropping a bill into an offering bucket, or adding your beautiful voice to the church choir, or even printing out the programs can't be the extent of your gift giving. Share. Expend energy. Spend some time. It will make Him smile and enhance your walk together. And I promise you, God won't forget.

119   GIVE HIM YOU

"Therefore, I urge you, brothers and sisters, in view of God's mercy, to offer your bodies as a living sacrifice, holy and pleasing to God—this is your true and proper worship. Do not conform to the pattern of this world but be transformed by the renewing of your mind. Then you will be able to test and approve what God's will is—His good, pleasing, and perfect will."

— Romans 12:1-2 (NIV)

The best gift you can give God on a daily basis is you. When you give Him you, everything else comes with it. There is a wedding tradition called "giving the bride away." The concept dates back to a time where women were considered property and the father received a dowry for her and gave her over to the groom. More than that, the father was relinquishing is loving responsibility over his daughter and gave those responsibilities to a man who he believed would lovingly care for her in the same way. But God has created us and has given us a free will to govern ourselves. We sold ourselves out to Satan, but Jesus has purchased us back. We are now to be the ones who give ourselves away as we become joined to Him in holy covenant.

Paul writes that we are to present our bodies a living sacrifice. Not like the dead animals mankind presented before to cover our sins. We are alive and able to serve Him in amazing ways. So, we present our bodies. We make a present of our bodies. When you just give something away there is no real concern about its condition or presentation. But, when you present the gift, when you make it a present, it matters to you what it looks like and how it is given. You do it with care because the preparation and presentation of the gift is part of the love behind the present. It shows that person how much they are valued, and how important it is for them to lovingly accept what you have carefully offered.

Today, as you spend time with God, make a present of yourself. Show that you care how you are presented and what you are presenting. Vow to work on your health, your appearance, your fitness, and nutrition. Vow to offer Him a holy body, free from addiction, sexual sin, destructive behaviors, and leftover energy. It is your reasonable service to the One who presented His body for you-blameless, sinless, guiltless, and whole. For God so loved He gave and because He gave, we give. Give Him you.

Naida M. Parson, Ph.D

120 RECEIVE GIFTS FROM HIM

"The king asked, "Is there no one still alive from the house of Saul to whom I can show God's kindness?" Ziba answered the king, "There is still a son of Jonathan; he is lame in both feet." "Where is he?" the king asked. Ziba answered, "He is at the house of Makir son of Ammiel in Lo Debar." So, King David had him brought from Lo Debar, from the house of Makir son of Ammiel. When Mephibosheth son of Jonathan, the son of Saul, came to David, he bowed down to pay him honor. David said, "Mephibosheth!" "At your service," he replied. "Don't be afraid," David said to him, " for I will surely show you kindness for the sake of your father Jonathan. I will restore to you all the land that belonged to your grandfather Saul, and you will always eat at my table." Mephibosheth bowed down and said, "What is your servant, that you should notice a dead dog like me?""

– 2 Samuel 9:3-8 (NIV)

Some of us don't receive well. We get stuck in our dysfunctional ways of life and don't receive the love, joy, and peace that God has given. We don't receive the blessing, or the ministry, or the miracle because of feeling unworthy or because we don't know how to walk in the great things God has provided. God is a giver. He is a lover, so He is a giver. Some people are willing to give of their gifts and talents to God along with their time and finances. But they have a difficult time accepting and receiving the things that God wants to give them. Gift giving must go both ways. In walking with God and developing a love relationship with Him, we must learn to take what is so lovingly given.

King David was a man after God's own heart. He had a great capacity to love, and when he became king, he remembered his love for his best friend Jonathan. He loved, so he wanted to give. When he found Jonathan's son Mephibosheth, David wanted to give him the best life possible. But Mephibosheth had a hard time receiving it. He had no problem giving David honor, but when David wanted to honor him in return, he only could see himself as a useless lame son of a dead prince and grandson of a rejected king. Like God, David's desire to bless Mephibosheth had to do with who he belonged to. God wants to give to us His best gifts because He loves us, and equally because of Who we belong to. We are in Christ and because of Him there are gifts and blessings that it is God's good pleasure to give us.

When God gives you gifts, receive them. If He gives you love, receive it, and allow yourself to be loved. If He gives you joy, receive it, and refuse to live in depression. If He gives you peace, received it, and reject all feelings of fear and anxiety. If He gives you forgiveness, receive it, and don't live in condemnation. This is a relationship. Make sure the gift giving goes both ways. Receive joy. Be happy. Accept the gift. Receive peace. Calm down. Have fun. Receive love. Embrace God and His people. Receive forgiveness. Forgive yourself. Start over. Begin behaving like a person who is tremendously loved. Ask Him today what gift He has given that your life doesn't reflect. Then, receive it with joy.

121 SERVE THE LORD WITH GLADNESS

"Make a joyful noise unto the Lord, all ye lands. Serve the Lord with gladness: come before His presence with singing. Know ye that the Lord He is God: it is He that hath made us, and not we ourselves; we are His people, and the sheep of His pasture."

— Psalms 100:1-3 (KJV)

Another way to express your love for God is to offer Him acts of service. Every day, ask Him what you can do for Him. Most of the time it will be things He would love for you to do for others. Jesus said that whatever we do for the least of His people we are doing for Him. There are prayers that are going up to Him every day from people who need help, or encouragement, or who need to hear the good news of Jesus Christ. Someone right now is praying for a miracle, or an answer and you are the person God can send to meet that need. When we do that, He is pleased and feels our love.

The psalmist in our scripture today encourages us to serve the Lord with gladness. There is so much joy in serving God! No one wants the person serving them to do it with complaints and a bitter attitude. Who wants service that seems like a bother or an imposition? And that's from people we don't even know, like a waiter, or mechanic, or store clerk. We would rather go to another restaurant or business than to be treated as if serving us ruined their day. But, when it is someone who is supposed to love you, especially when you have been so giving and overly gracious to them, it is that much more disheartening. We are to serve the Lord with gladness. He is God! He made us. We didn't make ourselves and there is nothing we can do for ourselves without Him.

So today, in your prayer time with God, ask Him what act of service He would like you to do. He may put someone on your mind to call. He may have you share financially, or buy food, or help pay a bill. He may point someone out to you and have you go speak to them, or He may remind you of a church project that could use your help. And when you have a sense of what God wants you to do, do it with gladness, excellence, and love.

122 JESUS IS AT YOUR SERVICE

"He came to Simon Peter, who said to Him, "Lord, are You going to wash my feet?"
Jesus replied, "You do not realize now what I am doing, but later you will understand."
"No," said Peter, "You shall never wash my feet." Jesus answered, "Unless I wash you,
you have no part with Me." "Then, Lord," Simon Peter replied, "not just my feet but
my hands and my head as well!""

– John 13:6-9 (NIV)

As with all the Love Languages, acts of service must go both ways. Sometimes we feel guilty for asking for things we need. Sometimes our pride and self-sufficiency keep us from allowing God to do things for us. You may think that most people's prayers are filled with "give me, give me", or "do this for me and then do that"! I guess that is true for people who have an immature relationship with God. Those who have matured beyond being self-centered may feel that asking for things from God constantly is a sign of selfishness and greed.

But God delights in doing things for His children. He longs for you to let Him do things for you. It doesn't mean you are immature and selfish. It means that you understand you are totally dependent on Him. It also means that you understand Him well and you know how much He delights in doing the things His children need. Peter learned this the hard way. Jesus wanted to share His love by washing His disciples' feet. This was a task for the lowest servant in the house. None of them felt inferior to any of the others evidently, so no one washed anyone's feet. Instead, they wanted to figure out who would be the greatest. Jesus showed them the depth of His love and then wanted to teach them a lesson in humility. But it was mostly about love. Love and service go together. He loves us and so He has no problem doing acts of service.

What is it Jesus can do for you today? What act of service do you need? A bill paid? A location on your wayward child? A miracle for you or your family? Do you need Him to open a door of opportunity for you? Someone is already shooting down this type of prayer. Maybe you feel unworthy. Don't worry about it. You are. Maybe you feel it was your mistake that got you here. Most likely it was. Maybe you feel others need it more. I'm sure they do. But you serve a God who wants to serve you. Ask Him to do what you need Him to do. He would love to be at your service.

Naida M. Parson, Ph.D

123 FAITH AND FAVOR

"On the third day a wedding took place at Cana in Galilee. Jesus' mother was there, and Jesus and His disciples had also been invited to the wedding. When the wine was gone, Jesus' mother said to Him, "They have no more wine." "Woman, why do you involve Me?" Jesus replied. "My hour has not yet come." His mother said to the servants, "Do whatever He tells you.""

– John 2:1-5 (NIV)

One lady who wasn't shy about asking our Savior for acts of service was His own mother. She was at a wedding with Him where the host ran out of wine. This would have been an embarrassment for her friend, and evidently it was a pretty big deal because she asked the Son of God for a favor. She asked Him to perform an act of service. I can imagine His frustration of being asked to work a miracle before His time. And then, it was a miracle that wasn't even life changing. It was a simple act of service asked of Someone who could do anything.

I wonder if He prayed to His Father to get permission and His Father simply said, "listen to Your mother." But what is more intriguing is that she had the nerve to ask. Maybe it was because she had the two things she needed to get her miracle: faith and favor. She knew who her Son was and that He had the power to do something about this thing she was so concerned about. And she knew that the relationship she had with Him put her in the position of favor. For whatever reason, she ignored His objection and made a faith move. She told the servants to do whatever He said, and she got her miracle that day.

Never be afraid to ask God for a favor. After all, you are walking together, and acts of service is one way He loves on you. Move in faith knowing that He can do so much more than you can ask, think, or imagine. And then move in favor knowing that if it's good for you, and if it's something you are deeply concerned about, He would love to do it for you. So, what do you need from God today? What do you have faith for because you certainly have His favor?

124 JUST DO IT

"The word of the Lord came to Jonah son of Amittai: "Go to the great city of Nineveh and preach against it, because its wickedness has come up before Me." But Jonah ran away from the Lord and headed for Tarshish. He went down to Joppa, where he found a ship bound for that port. After paying the fare, he went aboard and sailed for Tarshish to flee from the Lord."

– Jonah 1:1-3 (NIV)

When you ask God what you can do for Him today, listen for His voice and if He asks you to do something for Him, just do it. Don't hesitate. When you get the impression in your spirit, or get a clear instruction from Him, be willing and ready to do whatever He says. That is how you love on Him. That is how you worship Him. That is how you walk with Him and stay in step.

Don't be like Jonah. Jonah got an instruction from God and didn't like the act of service God required. Instead of packing up and going to the city of Ninevah, he went the opposite way. His disobedience almost cost him his life. God came after His disobedient preacher, and he ended up being thrown off his getaway ship. He landed in the belly of a great fish until he was ready to cooperate.

God most likely won't come after you that hard unless what He is asking you to do is such a big part of His plan that He can't let you back out. But He will go after you. Going after you is a testament to His great love, not just for the people who need you, but for you as well. Like a parent would a child, He will come after you. But He shouldn't have to. If He asks you to do something today, just do it. Love Him enough to do it just because He asked you to. That is the kind of relationship we strive to have with our Father. One of honor, respect, and obedience. This is easier said than done, but love will find a way, just like Jesus found a way to get it done when our world so desperately needed Him. The world needs you, too. Just do it.

Naida M. Parson, Ph.D

125 WHY IS IT A PROBLEM?

"Jesus looked at him and loved him. "One thing you lack," He said. "Go, sell everything you have and give to the poor, and you will have treasure in heaven. Then come, follow Me." At this the man's face fell. He went away sad because he had great wealth."

– Mark 10:21-22 (NIV)

I'm sure that when we hesitate to perform acts of service, God asks, "why should it be a problem for you to do things for Me?" Like anyone in a love relationship, we want to know that the person we love is as dedicated to our happiness as we are to theirs. God is absolutely dedicated to our happiness. He gave us the very best He had in His Son Jesus. Then, He meets our daily needs and a lot of our wants. So, why would it be a problem to perform acts of service for Him?

It's an issue the rich young ruler had to face. He came to Jesus seeking the key to eternal life. He listened intently to see what Jesus would tell him. But the answer he got was way too much for him to easily do. Jesus asked him to sell his great possessions, give the money to the poor, and then come and follow Him. He went away sorrowful because what he had was more important to him than what Jesus had to offer. But, more than that, his love for Jesus wasn't nearly strong enough.

When God asks you for acts of service, you may have to wrestle with how you really feel about Him. What if He asks you to do something embarrassing? What if He asks you to do something difficult? What if He asks you to do something time consuming or sacrificial? Do you love yourself, your comforts, your reputation, your money, or your precious time more than you love the God who has given you all the above? We all struggle to do God's will and we all must wrestle with our why? Why is it a problem to perform service for God? Talk to Him about that today. Share with Him your hesitations. Settle the issue so that you can honor your relationship and prove that nothing He wants from you will ever be withheld again.

126 IT GOES BOTH WAYS

"Greater love has no one than this: to lay down one's life for one's friends. You are My friends if you do what I command. I no longer call you servants because a servant does not know his master's business. Instead, I have called you friends, for everything that I learned from My Father I have made known to you. You did not choose Me, but I chose you and appointed you so that you might go and bear fruit—fruit that will last—and so that whatever you ask in My name the Father will give you."

– John 15:13-16 (NIV)

Have you ever been in a one-sided relationship? It's where you do all the calling, and all the giving, and all the arrangements for quality time. It's where you love more than they do. It's where you put forth all the effort and they just enjoy the chase. It's the kind of relationship you can never feel secure in because you know that you want them a lot more than they want you. But you keep pursuing in hopes that they might change their mind and maybe see how special you are eventually. I would say that a person who stays in that kind of one-sided relationship has a low self-esteem problem.

But that is just where God finds Himself with us. And no, God has absolutely no problem with His self-esteem. He just has such an impossible and tremendous love for us that He cannot let us go without a fight. So, He does the calling. He does the pursuing. He does the nudging. He came after us hard by giving His only Son and He keeps pursuing us through the Holy Spirit. Still, Jesus lets us know that the Godhead is not happy in a one-sided relationship. Jesus said to His disciples that He was laying down His life for His friends, and that if they were only servants, He would not share with them His heart and the plans of God. But because the relationship went both ways-He loved them, and they loved Him-He has shared with them everything the Father shared with Him.

Today, enhance your walk with God by doing something you would do with a friend, or saying something that you would say to a friend. God doesn't want to be in a one-sided relationship. When you praise Him, He wants to affirm you. When you give your gifts to Him, He wants to give gifts to you. When He does things for you, He would love for you to do things for Him. When He wants to spend time with you, He wants you to sometimes initiate spending time with Him. Servants just do what they are told with no relationship required. But friends are together because they want to be. Jesus has called you friend. Make sure that goes both ways.

Naida M. Parson, Ph.D

127 QUALITY TIME

"That evening after sunset the people brought to Jesus all the sick and demon possessed. The whole town gathered at the door, and Jesus healed many who had various diseases. He also drove out many demons, but He would not let the demons speak because they knew who He was. Very early in the morning, while it was still dark, Jesus got up, left the house, and went off to a solitary place, where He prayed. Simon and his companions went to look for Him, and when they found Him, they exclaimed: "Everyone is looking for You!"

– Mark 1:32-37 (NIV)

The next most important thing you will ever do in life, after accepting the Lord as your personal Savior, is to spend quality time with Him. You have heard it a thousand times I'm sure, "Christianity is not a religion… it is a relationship". Being a Christian means being in a loving and ever developing intimate relationship with God through Jesus Christ. The relationship is so intimate that His Holy Spirit actually comes to live inside you and the walk with God begins.

Jesus is our ultimate example of how to walk with God. We don't have much information on Enoch's experience. We don't know what it was like day by day. But we do have that example in Jesus. Jesus had a habit of pulling away from everyone to spend quality time with His Father. Sometimes it would go on all night. In this scripture, He had just done some great ministry. There was still so much more to be done that the people were searching for Him. Yet Jesus so valued His time with God, He left ministry to be with God. Our ministry to people should flow out of our one-on-one relationship with God. This kind of relationship takes time. Jesus understood that. Repeatedly, especially after strenuous days of ministry, Jesus would leave it all for His personal, private time with God.

God wants quality time with us … daily. This includes time in prayer, reading, and worship. He wants time that is only about learning Him and loving on Him. He is asking for time when it's quiet and undisturbed by distractions, other people, and your own agenda. Walking with God requires quality time. So today, don't rush through your prayer. Pick a time when you can focus on Him and Him alone. Talk to Him and listen for Him. And do it often. Do it daily. This is the only real way to walk with God.

128 PRODUCTIVE TIME

"Remain in Me, as I also remain in you. No branch can bear fruit by itself; it must remain in the vine. Neither can you bear fruit unless you remain in Me. "I am the Vine; you are the branches. If you remain in Me and I in you, you will bear much fruit; apart from Me you can do nothing. If you do not remain in Me, you are like a branch that is thrown away and withers; such branches are picked up, thrown into the fire, and burned."

– John 15:4-6 (NIV)

Being productive in life is one of the perks of walking with God. When we are with Him daily, we get the opportunity to be involved in His activity in the world. God wants us to live a fruitful life. He has given us time, space, resources, and potential to do something with our lives on planet earth. Many scriptures in the Bible give us an indication that God has a bit of an attitude with anything, and anybody, that takes up space, but does not produce. His will is that we bear much fruit, meaning that we do something significant that has impact in this life and in eternity. The only way to do that is to allow Him to do it through you. Spending time with God daily is absolutely necessary.

Jesus gives the analogy of a vine and branches. If the branches stay connected to the vine, they will produce fruit. If they are cut away from the main vine they will eventually dry up and die, but certainly they will not produce fruit on their own. Everything needed to make fruit must flow from the main vine. Our daily quiet time, prayer time, and time in His word, are the ways we remain in Him. We hear from Him and He flows through us. As we obey what we hear from Him, we are producing what He wants to accomplish through us. Obeying Him is also abiding, or remaining, in Him. If He is going one direction and we don't move with Him, we haven't remained in Him. If we move in a direction that He has not authorized, then we aren't remaining in Him.

So, in your time with Him today, try to sense His will and His guidance. If you follow what He says, you will live a life of satisfying service to your Lord and His Kingdom. You will be able to look back and see fruit. You will have an eternal impact on this world. That impact may come through a mission, or a word to the nations, or through the classroom where you teach, or through the daily interactions with the kid that is in your house. Either way, it has to start and end with daily time with God. Walking with God is daily. It is imperative.

Naida M. Parson, Ph.D

129 PRACTICE HIS PRESENCE

"One thing I ask from the Lord, this only do I seek: that I may dwell in the house of the Lord all the days of my life, to gaze on the beauty of the Lord and to seek Him in His temple."

— Psalms 27:4 (NIV)

Walking with God moves far beyond your daily prayer time. As you get closer and more intimate with Him, you "tune in" to Him throughout your day. Think of it in the same way as if your very best friend spent the entire day with you. You wouldn't just speak to them in the morning and then go about your day and not look their way or say another word to them until the evening. You would speak to them all day. If they went to work with you, you would share and discuss what you're doing. Even if your activities took your attention for a while, you would drift back into conversations with them. You would talk more over lunch. You would discuss the day. You would share your meals, and your heart, from time to time. Throughout the day you would acknowledge the presence of your friend, and they would be talking, and sharing, and reacting to you as well.

King David had such a friendship with God. He was so elated to be in His presence that it became his one desire. Above anything else in life, if he had his choice of where he wanted to be, he would choose to dwell where God was. In his day, that was the house of the Lord. It was where he could, in a sense, gaze on the beauty of the Lord and find out more about Him. Maybe that's why he wanted to build God a grander temple. Maybe this psalm was partly his dream. One thing he desired, and decided to ask God for, was to just be with Him. We don't have to have a temple in our day. We have the honor of being able to be with God all day, every day. We just have to be aware of that blessing and intentional in our pursuit. We have to practice being aware of His presence and interacting with God all day.

Your task today is to practice the presence of God. He is constantly there, but if you don't practice making yourself aware of it, your relationship will feel distant. He is with you. He is in your head, and He knows your thoughts. He is in your car, and at your job. His hand is on you, even in your darkest moments. You may not understand how some things can happen if He is there, but since He is, just ask Him. Share your heart and allow Him to share His. Ask Him about anything and everything. David did. He said that some of it was way above his head! But he practiced the presence of God. If you will too, you will find a new intimacy with every passing day.

130 UNINTERRUPTED TIME

"And when you pray, do not be like the hypocrites, for they love to pray standing in the synagogues and on the street corners to be seen by others. Truly I tell you, they have received their reward in full. But when you pray, go into your room, close the door, and pray to your Father, Who is unseen. Then your Father, Who sees what is done in secret, will reward you."

– Matthew 6:5-6 (NIV)

We should have daily uninterrupted time with God. In this day of cell phones, television, social media, and video games, few people spend time face to face with the ones they love purely uninterrupted. And the truth is, we don't particularly like not having our loved one's full attention. It feels like we are not important. It feels like we are not significant. It feels like we are not truly being listened to or prioritized. When we are building relationship, we want uninterrupted time with the person we are interacting with. We want them to know us and truly appreciate our presence. Otherwise, are you ever really with me?

This scripture is from a sermon Jesus was preaching. He approaches the subject of prayer. He is actually talking about motive and how some of the religious elites were praying only to be seen. But in it He instructs us on how He would like us to approach the Father in prayer. "Go into your room and close the door and pray to your Father." Not out and about where people see you, but privately and secretly. This is not to say that we are not to pray wherever, and whenever, we can. But it does set us up for intimate, uninterrupted time with God that is away from everyone and everything else.

If you have not already done so by this portion of the book, choose a time that you can talk to God without interruption and not on the way to work, or while you're getting dressed, or in between yelling at the kids, or fixing dinner. Daily, find some time with God where you are not likely to be interrupted. Even if it's just fifteen minutes to focus on Him, and only Him. Make Him your priority. Show Him He is special and that nothing matters more than knowing Him, loving on Him, and being in His presence. Uninterrupted time with God. Find that time today. He is worth it. He is worthy of it.

Naida M. Parson, Ph.D

131 UNDISTRACTED TIME

"As Jesus and His disciples were on their way, He came to a village where a woman named Martha opened her home to Him. She had a sister called Mary, who sat at the Lord's feet listening to what He said. But Martha was distracted by all the preparations that had to be made. She came to Him and asked, "Lord, don't you care that my sister has left me to do the work by myself? Tell her to help me!" "Martha, Martha," the Lord answered, "you are worried and upset about many things, but few things are needed—or indeed only one. Mary has chosen what is better, and it will not be taken away from her.""

– Luke 10:38-42 (NIV)

Our lives are full of distractions. Our jobs, our children, our love interests … bills, tasks, emergencies … church work, community events, extended family. And then, of course, there are the pleasures of life that distract us even more. When we are walking with God, anything that takes our attention can get us off the track of His divine will for us. Consequently, we should have daily undistracted time with Him. Uninterrupted time means that we choose a time and place where we will not be interrupted by people or events. Undistracted time speaks more to the mental things that take our attention from Him, as well as other things we are doing at the same time we are trying to focus on God. You can be distracted even when you haven't been interrupted.

This is the second time we are visiting this story in this devotional, but it's the best example to make the point. Mary, Martha, and Lazarus are in their home, and it seems they had Jesus to themselves. The Bible says that the disciples were in town with Him, but it didn't say Martha opened her home to "them." It said she opened her home to "Him." Since Mary was at His feet listening to Him, we can assume they weren't being interrupted. But Martha was distracted. Maybe she was trying to listen as Jesus was talking, but there were other things to do. Martha was attempting to multitask, I suppose. Mary, however, had laser focus at the feet of Jesus as He shares with them. Martha was distracted by all the preparations that had to be made when you have an impromptu house guest. She felt her sister should have been helping out, but Jesus laid down a very important principle. When it comes to walking with God, only one thing is absolutely necessary: undistracted time with God.

Today and every day, choose to have some time that you can be in the presence of God without being interrupted by people and distracted by life. Set your time, even if it's a few minutes, where nothing will interrupt you. Then set your mind and your environment where nothing will distract you. Listen only to Jesus through His word, or meditation, or worship, or however you hear His voice. Lots of things are important, but only one is necessary for your life. Choose the best part like Mary did. Today.

132 UNDISTURBED TIME

"Immediately Jesus made the disciples get into the boat and go on ahead of Him to the other side, while He dismissed the crowd. After He had dismissed them, He went up on a mountainside by Himself to pray. Later that night, He was there alone,"

– Matthew 14:22-23 (NIV)

In order to make the absolute best out of your walking with God, in order to have the ultimate Enoch experience, your goal and your commitment should be to have daily uninterrupted, undistracted, and undisturbed time with Him. Uninterrupted means that you choose a time where your fellowship with Him will not be interrupted by people, or other events, or tasks. Undistracted time means that mentally and physically nothing else is taking your attention and you can focus on Him and hear what He is saying to you. You can be uninterrupted, but still be distracted. You can also be giving God your full attention, but then be interrupted.

And you can also pick a great time to be with God with no distractions or interruptions but disturb that time with negative and unnecessary conversation and concerns. Have you ever had a conversation ruin a good time? This happens in marriage often. The husband and wife go off together for a relationship building rendezvous and spend the time talking about the children, and the bills, and the household repairs! No wonder Jesus got away often to spend undisturbed time with God. He dismissed the crowd. He dismissed the disciples. He found himself a mountainside and went there to pray alone and stayed there a while, undisturbed.

When Jesus got through spending that time with God, He felt good enough to go walking on water! When you spend time with God today, don't disturb it with your troubles and fears. Don't discuss your frustrations and failures. Have some time with God that is peaceful, and loving, and worshipful, and pleasant. Don't ruin a good time with disturbing conversation. There will be plenty of time during the day to go into all those things. Take some time just for fellowship and a relationship building rendezvous. You may come out of it ready to walk on water!

133 SCHEDULE TIME

"Now when Daniel learned that the decree had been published, he went home to his upstairs room where the windows opened toward Jerusalem. Three times a day he got down on his knees and prayed, giving thanks to his God, just as he had done before. Then these men went as a group and found Daniel praying and asking God for help."

– Daniel 6:10-11 (NIV)

Most of the things that are extremely important to us are scheduled into our days. If there is something you can't miss, you put it on your calendar, in your planner, or on your phone. You even have your phone alert you so you don't forget. If indeed walking with God is your priority, you should make having uninterrupted, undistracted, and undisturbed time with Him a priority. Schedule it, if you must. You may need a strategy to make it happen. Don't leave it to chance. Remember that you have a demonic enemy who will do everything he can to make sure this time doesn't happen on a regular basis.

Daniel knew this all too well. The devil constantly stirred up opposition to Daniel's prayer life. At one time, they actually made it illegal for him to pray. The penalty was death in the lion's den. But Daniel had God on his schedule. Three times a day he had his time, his place, and his direction for prayer. Nothing else was allowed to alter that time. He was known for it. Everyone seemed to know exactly where he would be. Does your family know your prayer time? Do your friends know not to call you then? Have you made it priority enough that others can set their watch by it?

Today, begin to look at your schedule. Develop a strategy to have some time that belongs to God. Of course, you will commune with Him throughout the day. And, of course, things will come up that may cause some adjustment. Maybe you're not a structured kind of person, but when it's important, we all schedule things. Especially when it involves other people meeting us there. God wants to meet with you daily. It's important to Him. It's important to your walk with Him. He would love it to be important to you, too. Can He get on your schedule?

Naida M. Parson, Ph.D

134 STEAL TIME

"Now there was a Pharisee, a man named Nicodemus who was a member of the Jewish ruling council. He came to Jesus at night and said, "Rabbi, we know that You are a teacher who has come from God. For no one could perform the signs You are doing if God were not with Him.""

– John 3:1-2 (NIV)

As much as it is important to have some scheduled time with God, it is so pleasant, and rewarding, to steal some time when you can. There was a television show where a couple who were not supposed to be together had to steal time with one another. One would say to the other, "one minute." Though the action was sinful, the sentiment was quite romantic. They were so into each other that just one minute in the same place, at the same time, without a word being spoken, heightened their intimacy. It brought them into each other's world and connected them again, even if it was just for one minute.

Nicodemus sought to steal a moment with Jesus one night. He was not supposed to be with Him. He was a Pharisee. His team was not team Jesus at all! He would have had a hard time being open and sincere in front of everyone I suppose, so he came to Jesus by night. He came to steal a moment with Him, ask Him questions, and connect with Him even if it was just for a moment. Because he stole some time with Jesus, he got some revelations that no one else had heard. Jesus spent sweet time with him, even though it was unscheduled.

Throughout your day today, during an unexpected break, or in your car, between a meeting, while in your room changing for your next event, on the drive home from work, while waiting on an appointment that's running late, on a plane ride, or waiting on your bus, steal moments with God. Say a prayer. Ask a question. Thank Him for something. Read a scripture and listen for a revelation. Just look up and say, "I love You." Imagine yourself at His throne for a moment of worship. One minute. Steal it away from your day. As you develop an intimacy with God, you will find those moments to be some of the best memories you will ever have.

135 TOUCH HIM

"When one of the Pharisees invited Jesus to have dinner with him, He went to the Pharisee's house and reclined at the table. A woman in that town who lived a sinful life learned that Jesus was eating at the Pharisee's house, so she came there with an alabaster jar of perfume. As she stood behind Him at His feet weeping, she began to wet His feet with her tears. Then she wiped them with her hair, kissed them and poured perfume on them."

– Luke 7:36-38 (NIV)

The love language that is the most difficult to share with God is probably Physical Touch. When Jesus was here in the flesh, the people who walked with Him could literally touch Him. Jesus was a man who was open and willing to touch and be touched. He allowed people to touch Him who weren't supposed to, like the woman who had a blood issue that made her unclean, or the children whose mothers brought them to Jesus, and the disciples attempted to forbid them. Then there were those He touched that He wasn't supposed to touch, like the leper and a dead man's bier. You can't touch God physically, but you can touch Him and be touched by Him spiritually.

This scripture revisits a woman we saw before in this book. The woman in this story was so grateful to be forgiven, accepted, and considered by Jesus, that she was moved to tearful worship. She cried at His feet, and when her tears wet His feet, she touched Him. She dried His feet with her hair and put expensive perfumed ointment on them. The outward touch was simply an expression of a spiritual touch. He touched her issue, and she touched His heart. Had they never made physical contact, they still touched each other in spirit. When you have an experience with God, a true spiritual encounter, it will feel like He has reached out His hand and touched you, and when you respond to His touch with worship and gratitude, you will feel like you have touched Him back.

Today as you enter His presence through your prayer time, open your spirit to be touched by Him. Add it to your prayer. "Lord, touch me and let me experience You in a whole new way. Let me literally feel Your presence. I reach for You through my spirit man. Help me to connect with You intimately and know I've been touched by the hand of God". Some describe it as a warmth. Some as a chill. Some cry and some have even been known to laugh. Some feel compelled to raise or wave their hands. And some just sense His presence. But He can truly be touched, and He most certainly can touch you back.

Naida M. Parson, Ph.D

136 IMAGINE IT!

"And a woman was there who had been subject to bleeding for twelve years. She had suffered a great deal under the care of many doctors and had spent all she had, yet instead of getting better she grew worse. When she heard about Jesus, she came up behind Him in the crowd and touched His cloak, because she thought, "If I just touch His clothes, I will be healed.""

– Mark 5:25-28 (NIV)

The human imagination is powerful. Most of the amazing things we have become accustomed to like flying, microwaves, smart phones, and the World Wide Web started off in someone's imagination. Our human imagination has been used for everything from improving athletic performance to healing terminal disease. Our imagination is God given and it can produce in us the same emotions as the real experience. So, although you cannot physically touch God, you can use your imagination to focus your experience with God.

The woman who HAD an issue of blood for years actually touched Jesus in her mind before she touched Him with her hand. After she heard of Him, she most likely imagined the whole scenario in her mind. She said within herself that if she could just touch His clothes, she would be healed. She heard, she came, and she touched because she thought. She imagined what could happen and then took the chance to do what she had already seen. That reminds me of how God does things. He speaks things that are not as though they were and then they are! God has a great imagination. His thoughts are His plans. That's why the scripture that says, "I know the thoughts I think toward you" (Jeremiah 29:11) can be translated "I know the plans I have for you." We are in His image so we can use our minds to touch Him.

Use your imagination today to touch God and to experience physical touch in a way that builds your intimacy with Him. Imagine coming before His throne after entering His gates with thanksgiving and His courts with praise. Kneel before Him in your mind and reach out to touch Him. Maybe reach up, or lay your head on His feet, or even embrace Him like a child would their father. It is your time and your space to be intimate and touch your God. You can also image Him touching you back. Perhaps laying His hand on you like Biblical fathers blessed their sons. You can't touch God with your hands, but you can touch Him and use that love language by your God given imagination. It certainly works for me. Try that today and add it to your daily time with God.

# 137 SOMETHING HAPPENS WITH HIS TOUCH

"When she heard about Jesus, she came up behind Him in the crowd and touched His cloak, because she thought, "If I just touch His clothes, I will be healed." Immediately her bleeding stopped, and she felt in her body that she was freed from her suffering. At once Jesus realized that power had gone out from Him. He turned around in the crowd and asked, "Who touched My clothes?""

– Mark 5:27-30 (NIV)

Though it may take imagination to touch God physically, we know we are able to touch God spiritually. We are spirit beings, and this is the way we must interact with God. However, when you "touch" Him in your spirit, that will often have a physical manifestation. I have heard many people express how they feel when they have been touched by God. One song writer describes it like this:

He touched me
Oh, He touched me.
And oh, the joy that floods my soul.
Something happened and now I know,
He touched me and made me whole.

This would be the testimony of this woman who pressed through the crowd to touch Jesus. Except, in this case she touched Him instead of Him touching her. Love languages must go both ways. When we exchange touch with God in our spirit man, or with the use of the imagination, a true touch happens and it has the ability to heal you, settle you, comfort you, transform you, or even break you. You may cry, smile, laugh, have a feeling of total peace, or feel a chill that sets your hair on edge and gives you goose bumps! Passionate cultures may scream out, dance, or wave their hands. Milder cultures may quietly raise their hands in adoration. But when you're touched by God, you will often physically feel Him.

So, as you pray and spend your personal time with God today, as you walk with Him throughout your day, reach out to touch Him. Use your imagination to embrace Him. Allow Him, and ask Him, to touch you back. If you need to be healed physically, spiritually, mentally, or emotionally ask Him to touch those places in your life. There are few things more intimate than a gentle touch from the One you love. Reach out to Him now and let His touch make you whole.

Naida M. Parson, Ph.D

138 TOUCH HIM IN WORSHIP

"Six days before the Passover, Jesus came to Bethany, where Lazarus lived, whom Jesus had raised from the dead. Here a dinner was given in Jesus' honor. Martha served, while Lazarus was among those reclining at the table with Him. Then Mary took about a pint of pure nard, an expensive perfume; she poured it on Jesus' feet and wiped His feet with her hair. And the house was filled with the fragrance of the perfume."

– John 12:1-3 (NIV)

Touching God can be achieved in worship. As you spend time with Him in prayer and meet Him in your mind at His throne, reach out and touch Him in worship. You may imagine yourself kneeling before Him and reaching out to touch Him. You may imagine Him reaching down as He accepts your worship and touching you back. Worship is appreciating Who He is above what He has done. Worship is loving Him purely for the God He is. This is the best time to share with Him physical touch as you worship in His presence.

As far as we can tell in the scriptures, it appears that Jesus was anointed with perfume on two occasions. One woman was a sinner and unnamed. But nearer to the time of His crucifixion, Mary of Bethany performed this same act of worship. She poured the perfume on His feet and wiped them with her hair. She did it purely out of love. Love made her worship, and in her worship, she touched Him. Words couldn't express everything she must have wanted to say to Him. He was her friend, her teacher, her Lord and the One Who brought her brother back from the dead. She wanted to touch Him in a show of love that was pure worship.

Every day that you spend time with God, find yourself in worship. Tell Him Who He is to you. Express to Him the attributes you love most about Him. Acknowledge Who He is in the universe and eternity. And, as you celebrate and recognize Him for who He is, use your imagination to reach out, reach up, or reach across to Him. Touch Him in worship and you'll touch Him in a way that goes deeper than any flesh and blood touch. And He will touch you back. Practice this again today and let it be a part of your prayer routine as you walk with God.

139 TOUCH HIM IN THE SPIRIT

"And I will ask the Father, and He will give you another Advocate to help you and be with you forever— the Spirit of Truth. The world cannot accept Him because it neither sees Him nor knows Him. But you know Him, for He lives with you and will be in you. I will not leave you as orphans; I will come to you. Before long, the world will not see Me anymore, but you will see Me. Because I live, you also will live. On that day you will realize that I am in My Father, and you are in Me, and I am in you."

– John 14:16-20 (NIV)

Since we cannot touch God with flesh and blood, we must connect with Him through our spirit. When we accept Jesus and we are born again, the Holy Spirit comes into our human spirit and makes it alive again. From that point on, we are connected to God through our spirits. This relationship is spiritual. This walking with God is spiritual. Our spirit is the part of us that is totally God conscious. It is where the walk with God is done.

When Jesus was about to return to heaven, He let His disciples know that He would not leave them as orphans even though He would no longer be there in flesh and blood. He would send them another Advocate, another Comforter, another Teacher, another form of His divine presence. God, the Holy Spirit, would come and live with them and in them. Jesus still lives. Jesus is in God. We are in Jesus. The Holy Spirit is in us. So, He leads us, teaches us, guides us, and corrects us all from inside our spirit.

Today, determine to be more aware of the presence of the Holy Spirit within you. Be aware of His leading and guiding you. Know His touch in your spirit. Pay attention to His warnings, and urgings, and unctions. This is the equivalent to physical touch in the earth realm. You will literally feel Him often. That touch may make you feel at peace, or cry, or shiver, or feel deep emotion. There is a way to touch God. It's through the indwelling of His Holy Spirit.

Naida M. Parson, Ph.D

140 WALK WITH HIM INSIDE

"If we live in the Spirit, let us also walk in the Spirit."

– Galatians 5:25 (KJV)

Walking effectively with God requires that we learn to walk in the Spirit. Unfortunately, most people have no idea what that means. God lives inside of the believer through the indwelling Holy Spirit which you receive when you accept Jesus. That Spirit fills you up when you ask in faith for Him to fill you like He did the disciples in Acts Chapter 2 and Chapter 5. The Holy Spirit is inside of you, so walk with Him inside. It is there that He leads you, guides you, nudges you, and reveals things to you. So, walking in the Spirit means obeying those nudges and leadings.

The Bible speaks of an unction from the Spirit. This may come in the form of a feeling. Something like an intuition. You may be getting ready to accept a new job, but it doesn't feel right to you. You feel uncomfortable when you enter the building. You pray for the guidance of the Holy Spirit and you just don't feel right about saying yes to the job. It may seem perfect for you and the money may be great, but deep inside you know it's not right. Consequently, you turn it down and suddenly feel a calm and a peace. That is walking in the Spirit. It's knowing that God is walking with you every day from the inside. It's learning to be sensitive and more increasingly aware that He is guiding you. It's feeling for Him as you walk. Feel for His encouragements and His rebukes. Reach out to Him and get a feel for what He is saying to you.

Today in your prayer time, ask the Holy Spirit to lead you from the inside all day. Be more aware of your inner feelings, especially when you need to make a decision. Some people don't believe that God cares about the small things that matter to us. But I think He does. So even if you feel a nudging from the inner part of you that leads you to go down one street instead of another, follow it. Get used to living with the assurance that God is inside of you and walk with Him inside.

141 LIVE FROM THE INSIDE OUT

"But you have an anointing from the Holy One, and all of you know the truth.

As for you, the anointing you received from Him remains in you, and you do not need anyone to teach you. But as His anointing teaches you about all things and as that anointing is real, not counterfeit—just as it has taught you, remain in Him."

— 1 John 2:20, 27 (NIV)

Since God is living inside you through His Holy Spirit, live from the inside out. No longer should all of your decisions come from your logical reasoning and external knowledge. The Holy Spirit is like the Central Intelligence Agency or the Federal Bureau of Investigation. These agencies give our government information that is used to make decisions that affect the country. They call that information, Intel. These agencies always have information others don't have. The things they know are considered secret and highly classified. When the government trusts the information, they make decisions accordingly.

The Bible says in these scriptures that we have an anointing from the Holy One. Some translations call it an unction. It is an inner supernatural presence of God that leads and teaches us what the will of God is for our lives. When we are filled with the Spirit and obey this unction, or anointing, we don't need anyone else to teach us. This doesn't mean there are not God ordained teachers and pastors that explain to us the word of God, but what it does mean is that you're never on your own to run your life. If there were no one else to depend on, you have an internal Intel that gives you information supernaturally. It's information that you may never have known if left to your own abilities and insights.

Today, determine to continue the pattern of being aware of the movement and communication of the Holy Spirit living inside you. Don't live by what you see, hear, or understand from the outside. Depend more and more on what you perceive and know from the inside. This is the ultimate act of walking with God and feeling for Him through His Spirit. Allow Him to teach you, guide you, and be your leader. He is your Lord. Hear Him and say yes. Live from the inside out.

Naida M. Parson, Ph.D

142 THIS IS THE WAY ... WALK IN IT

"Whether you turn to the right or to the left, your ears will hear a Voice behind you, saying, "This is the way; walk in it.""

– Isaiah 30:21 (NIV)

Walking with God requires that you figure out how to hear Him and simply obey His instructions. Use your imagination to put yourself in His presence and focus on just being with Him. That will give you the experience of God from the outside. Then, do all you can to learn how He guides you from that inner unction and "feel" Him from the inside. He will also speak to you through His Word, a timely word from another Christian or Christian leader, a Christian book, music, or even a movie with a spiritual theme. As you walk with Him over the years you will develop a wonderful relationship with Him that guides and directs your entire life. That is a great definition of walking with God: receiving guidance and direction from Him every day, for the duration of your life.

Some say He will only speak when you need to make a turn or a grand decision. Others say it is a daily conversation. In Isaiah, the prophet speaks of a time when the relationship between God and His people will be close enough for them to actually hear Him tell them what to do and where to turn. We will hear a Voice say, "this is the way, walk in it". That time is now. Jesus promised that the indwelling Holy Spirit would guide us into all truth. He promised He would never leave or forsake us. He promised we would not be left as orphans, but that He would come to us. It is up to us to put ourselves in the position to listen, hear, and obey.

So today, continue to sharpen your ability to feel God guiding you and shaping your decisions. Listen for His voice, read His word, and pray about every decision. See if you can spend a whole day in complete obedience. Don't do anything today that you sense is not God's will for your life. If you can do it for one day, you can do it for a week. If you can go all week walking in step with God, then you can do it for a month. Soon your walk with God will be a lifestyle and you will know the Enoch Experience.

143 ACCEPT CORRECTION

"And have you completely forgotten this word of encouragement that addresses you as a father addresses his son? It says, "My son, do not make light of the Lord's discipline, and do not lose heart when He rebukes you, because the Lord disciplines the one He loves, and He chastens everyone He accepts as His son." Endure hardship as discipline; God is treating you as His children. For what children are not disciplined by their father? If you are not disciplined—and everyone undergoes discipline—then you are not legitimate, not true sons and daughters at all. Moreover, we have all had human fathers who disciplined us, and we respected them for it. How much more should we submit to the Father of spirits and live! They disciplined us for a little while as they thought best; but God disciplines us for our good, in order that we may share in His holiness. No discipline seems pleasant at the time, but painful. Later on, however, it produces a harvest of righteousness and peace for those who have been trained by it."

— Hebrews 12:5-11 (NIV)

We live in a society where the rights of children have superseded the rights of the parents to raise them, discipline them, or hold them responsible. As a result, many children have no respect for authority. They tend to be self-centered and entitled and many will have a very difficult time taking care of themselves as adults. This was not God's design for His children. Though He walks with us in a loving, kind, and gentle relationship, He maintains the right and the responsibility to correct us and discipline us when we are going in the wrong direction or making poor decisions. A big part of walking with God is taking His correction and loving rebuke.

Here in the book of Hebrews, the writer reminds the readers that God is our Father and that we should not resist when He is disciplining us. When we go through hard times, it may be that God is using our circumstances to show us what can happen when we don't walk closely with Him. Sometimes our hardships reveal our character flaws and God uses the fallout to perfect us and show us the things in our lives that need to change. When this happens, He does not want us to be discouraged, or think that God has abandoned us. We are to take His correction as we would accept it from a good father. When our earthly parents corrected us, we may have been angry for a while and hurt by what they had to say, but we stayed in relationship with them because we understood their motive was love.

Naida M. Parson, Ph.D

If you are going through some difficulties in this season of your walk, ask God if there is something you need to correct or change. If something hard has happened to you lately, decide not to get bitter with God as if He has chosen to hurt you. Some things are just life and God never promised to exempt us from the difficult things in life. But some things are for the purpose of correction and when that is the case, simply accept the correction of God. It would be impossible to walk with Him if, at some time, He didn't influence us to stay in step with Him. If we were not rebellious by nature, we wouldn't need the chastisement. But since we have decided to walk God's way, we also must give Him the right to help us line up. Surrender your will to Him again, today.

144 LET HIM MENTOR YOU

"It was I who taught Ephraim to walk, taking them by the arms; but they did not realize it was I who healed them. I led them with cords of human kindness, with ties of love. To them I was like one who lifts a little child to the cheek, and I bent down to feed them."

— Hosea 11:3-4 (NIV)

One of the most productive and life changing relationships is the relationship between a mentor and a mentee. A mentor is more than a teacher. A mentor walks through a process of personal learning with the mentee. That process includes showing them how to do what the mentor has already done, then doing the task with them, and then being there to watch the mentee do it themselves. Mentors teach, train, demonstrate, watch, correct, encourage, hold accountable, supervise, support, model, explain and celebrate!

In your walk with God, He longs to be a mentor for you. This kind of relationship with His people is described in the book of Hosea. He refers to them as Ephraim, which is one of the tribes of Israel, but He is speaking to His chosen people. God is reminding them of how He has mentored them throughout their history and compares it to teaching a baby to walk, lifting them up, feeding them, loving them to health, and holding them by the arms as they take each step. This is what He wants to do for us as we walk with Him. Jesus came to earth in flesh and blood to walk where we walk, see what we see, hear what we hear, and feel what we feel. This way, He can truly mentor us because He has been where we are all endeavoring to go. He can be touched by the feelings we have because He has had them, too. He is the perfect mentor for us.

Today, begin to see God as your mentor. It doesn't matter where you are going, what field you are in, or what you're trying to accomplish. Let Him mentor your career. He knows your trade and its future, and yours too. Let Him mentor your marriage and parenting. He created you and them and He knows what is going to work for you all. Let Him mentor your finances. He is an expert at multiplying a little into a lot. Let Him mentor your ministry since it is His anyway. He will mentor anything from weight loss, to college, to starting a business. Release those things to His control and listen for His instruction. It will be life changing.

Naida M. Parson, Ph.D

145 LET HIM MOLD YOU

"This is the word that came to Jeremiah from the LORD: "Go down to the potter's house, and there I will give you My message." So, I went down to the potter's house, and I saw him working at the wheel. But the pot he was shaping from the clay was marred in his hands; so, the potter formed it into another pot, shaping it as seemed best to him. Then the word of the LORD came to me. He said, "Can I not do with you, Israel, as this potter does?" declares the LORD. "Like clay in the hand of the potter, so are you in My hand, Israel."

– Jeremiah 18:1-6 (NIV)

The longer you walk with God, the more you should be becoming who He has preordained for you to be. Remember, you were created on purpose and for a purpose. God has prescribed every detail of your looks, your personality, your talents, and your gifts. But in our disobedience and rebellion, we have strayed away from our intended shape and purpose. Sin has compromised us. Sin has damaged us. Sin has sent us on a tangent away from where God would have us to be. In this scripture about the potter's house, God uses the term, "marred in his hand." We are like a piece of clay in the hand of the potter that was supposed to be one pot but was marred, so it had to be shaped into something else.

The great thing about this scripture is that the clay never left the hand of the potter. As the potter's wheel goes around and around, the hand of the potter shapes it into what the potter sees it can be. Since we are clay with a free will, God as the Potter is asking us if we are willing to be molded. Can He not do with us as this potter has done with the clay? We are damaged by the sin in our lives, but as we continue our walk with God and stay in step with Him, He is continuing to mold us into an image of Himself as He lives through the uniqueness of who we are. In other words, He knows how He wants to be reflected in each of us and how He wants to use our gifts in His kingdom. He is the potter, and we are the clay. Allow Him to mold you.

Today, relax into the hands of the Potter. While you are on the potter's wheel it may seem as if you are going around and around the same issues, problems, situations, or circumstances. You may find yourself saying "this again?!?" But trust that the Potter's hands are on you, and even though it seems you are back in the same place, you are not in the same shape. He is molding you and each round is getting a different result. Rest in His capable hands. As you sense every change He is making in you, say "yes, Lord." I am clay in Your hands.

146 LET HIM PASTOR YOU

"The LORD is my shepherd, I lack nothing. He makes me lie down in green pastures, He leads me beside quiet waters, He refreshes my soul. He guides me along the right paths for His Name's sake. Even though I walk through the darkest valley, I will fear no evil, for You are with me; Your rod and Your staff, they comfort me."

— Psalm 23:1-4 (NIV)

You are on a wonderful lifetime walk with God! He is leading you from without and from within. He is mentoring you like a father. He is molding you like a potter. And here is the most beautiful connection of all; He is pastoring you like a shepherd. Jesus calls Himself the Good Shepherd who laid down His life for the sheep. The word "pastor" is rarely used in the bible. It is almost always translated "shepherd." Raising sheep was so common in that region that it was an easy analogy to make. Everyone understood. The shepherd was a caring and loving depiction of God's relationship with us. Shepherds walked with the sheep.

King David was originally a shepherd who walked with God. He gave us this great insight. He says that because of God shepherding us, pastoring us, we have no lack and no need to fear. We are led to places we can eat and drink, and we are protected and corrected. When walking with our Shepherd, He may lead us into some things that may not be to our liking. Still, we have no reason to fear because our Shepherd never leaves us nor forsakes us. God walks through this life with us at every turn, providing for us and guiding us through. He is taking us somewhere on this walk, and we should be excited to see what every great place has in store for us!

Today, begin to see God as your Pastor. Some of you reading this book have had a pastor and hopefully that has been a great experience. But, either way, your true Pastor is God Himself. Listen to His words, and His nudges, and be comforted that He is leading you to places where you will lack nothing and where you will have peace and safety. Get ready for Him to take you to some amazing places, both spiritually and naturally.

Naida M. Parson, Ph.D

147 LET HIM ADVISE YOU

"Blessed is the one who does not walk in step with the wicked or stand in the way that sinners take or sit in the company of mockers, but whose delight is in the law of the LORD, and who meditates on His law day and night. That person is like a tree planted by streams of water, which yields its fruit in season and whose leaf does not wither— whatever they do prospers."

– Psalm 1:1-3 (NIV)

In this day of television, internet, cable, satellites, social media, radio and videos, there are so many voices and opinions that bombard us constantly. Twenty-four hours a day, someone or something is telling us what to think, what to feel, and what to do. Add to that our families, our friends, counselors, authority figures and teachers. Unfortunately, they don't all tell us the same thing, nor do most of them tell us the truth. But if we don't trust anyone and don't take anyone's advice, we are left to our own limited and skewed understanding and that can spell disaster as well!

The first Psalm gives us the solution. If you want to be happy, fortunate, a.k.a. blessed, then do not walk in the footsteps of people who are ungodly. Do not stand in the same position of people who don't know God, nor should you follow their advice. Take the advice of God. Walking with God means seeking Him for the answers to whatever is challenging you in your life. Meditating on the written Word of God will answer every question and guide you in His will. Meditation is reading it and repeating it to yourself throughout the day. It means to let God give you revelation and understanding as you quote it over, and over again, or as you read it repeatedly. As you commit portions of the Bible to memory, it will come back to lead you when you most need it.

Today, you can start the habit of taking God's advice over anyone and anything else that tries to talk to you. There are godly people you can, and should, seek out to talk things over with. Counsel is great. But the godly counselor will always tell you what God has already said. Take His advice! What would Jesus do? What did He say? If you follow that, you will be like a tree by the water's edge. Flourishing. Fruitful. Successful. Blessed. When it's your season, nothing will be able to hinder you from what God has designed for you.

148 REMAIN "IN" HIM

"If you remain in Me and My words remain in you, ask whatever you wish, and it will be done for you. This is to My Father's glory, that you bear much fruit, showing yourselves to be My disciples. "As the Father has loved Me, so have I loved you. Now remain in My love. If you keep My commands, you will remain in My love, just as I have kept My Father's commands and remain in His love."

– John 15:7-10 (NIV)

Effectively walking with God requires total obedience. As we discussed earlier in this book, it may seem strange for an adult to be in a mutual loving relationship with someone who requires you to obey their every command. For your obedience to be equated with loving them seems absurd. But that is exactly what God is asking for. Disobeying God is equivalent to walking away from Him. The love part comes in because we truly are free willed beings. Your submissive act of obedience is the outward proof of your inward love. Being in step with Him, walking in harmony together, and getting the best out of the experience is completely reliant on keeping His commands.

We revisit this concept because in it we find the secret of living a productive life. The secret is to remain in Jesus. Early in the chapter, Jesus describes Himself as a True Vine and we are the branches. The idea is that everything that is in Him flows through us and then produces the desired result, or fruit. The branches cannot bear fruit by themselves. They must remain connected to the main vine. So, Jesus says we are to remain in Him and His word is to remain in us. He then lets us know what that means. If we keep His commands, we remain in His love. His commands are not hard or unreasonable. They are all for our good. Only He knows how we are made and for what purpose. His commands give us the best life possible.

So today, don't walk away from God through disobedience. Search for areas of your life where you have not been completely obedient. It may be in your prayer time, or in how you manage your finances, or your attitude at home, or an area of behavior that needs to change. Every time you bring one area under submission, find another one to tackle. I'm sure it will be a while before you run out. He will, of course, give you grace for wherever you fall short, but this is about loving Him and wanting to walk with Him. The fact that it makes you productive is just the added bonus. You and God can do great things together. Remain in Him.

Naida M. Parson, Ph.D

149 THIS WALK IS A COVENANT

"And he said: "LORD God of Israel, there is no God in heaven above or on earth below like You, who keep Your covenant and mercy with Your servants who walk before You with all their hearts."

— I Kings 8:23 (NKJV)

Staying in agreement with God is the goal of walking with Him. This point is repetitive because this walk is repetitive. It's daily. Every day you make the decision. You and God agree to walk together, and you cannot walk together unless you stay in agreement. We have agreed to meet with Him and let Him choose the route and the destination. It's not rocket science. If God is going right and you disagree and go left, then you have ceased to walk together. But more than that, there is a level of covenant and promise between you and God. You both have entered a spiritual contract. You both agree as to what is right, what is true, and what will be done with your life. Each person takes responsibility to uphold their end of the agreement. Our walk is more than a journey. It's a covenant.

In this scripture today, King Solomon is dedicating the temple he built for God. He has brought the Ark of the Covenant to the temple and God has already entered the Holy Place where He promised His presence would be with His people. At this point, Solomon makes this statement that God will keep covenant with those who walk before Him. He will keep His promises, His contract, His agreements with those on a walk with Him. The reason God shows up in this temple that Solomon and the people built was because of a sacred covenant He made with His people when they crafted the Ark after coming out of Egypt. God keeps His side of the covenant. Always. Every day you show up to walk with Him, He will show up and walk with you.

So today, renew your covenant with God. Agree with Him that being a Christian and living by His word is the route you will take. Being with Him in heaven for eternity is the agreed upon destination and the agreed upon time is now. What an honor it is to be invited to walk with your Father! The Creator of the universe asked you to come, and you have agreed. Walking with God is a covenant with wonderful promises and a destination that is out of this world. Take it seriously. He certainly does.

150 JUST ENJOY BEING TOGETHER

"His mouth is sweetness itself; he is altogether lovely. This is my beloved, this is my friend, daughters of Jerusalem."

– Song of Solomon 5:16 (NIV)

Oh, how wonderful it is to be in love! The thought of that person makes you smile. When you catch a glimpse of their profile your heart skips a beat. Their embrace feels like the comfort of home. When you are away from them you feel incomplete. You long for conversation, connection, and just their presence. And as the love grows through the seasons of life, they become more and more a part of you until you don't know where they end, and you begin. What an amazing experience it is to be in love!

The Song of Solomon tells a love story between Solomon and the love of his life (at least at the time). It is included in the Bible, not just because of its historical contribution, but as a representation of what the future relationship between Christ and the church would be like. She says of her love and friend that he is altogether lovely. We sing this same thing to Jesus. He is altogether lovely! We are to stay in awe of Him. But this is a two-way love story. He is also in love with us. He longs for conversation with us, for connection to us, and just to be in our presence.

Today, you and God can just enjoy being together. Just love on Him by staying in His presence for a while. Tell Him how you feel about Him. Tell Him that the word He speaks to you is sweetness itself. This is easier for women because it comes naturally. For men it may be more of a "bromance". Enjoy God like you're hanging out with your best friend or your closest brother. Just talk together. Walk together. Love the relationship and the fact that you are there for each other. Walking with God is all about relationship. He is your beloved. He is your friend.

Naida M. Parson, Ph.D

151 STAY GRATEFUL

"Give thanks to the Lord, for He is good. His love endures forever. Give thanks to the God of gods. His love endures forever. Give thanks to the Lord of lords: His love endures forever."

— Psalm 136:1-3 (NIV)

It is so easy to take God for granted. This term means that things others may hope to receive, you would consider automatically granted. You expect it to be there so completely that you don't ask for it anymore and you are not grateful either. Most of us fully expect to wake up tomorrow morning. We fully expect to live the rest of the day. We truly believe we are going to be around for Christmas and have already made plans. We are not grateful for time. Most of us believe we will continue to have access to food, air, and water, and so we consume it without thought. We stand, fully expecting to walk. We open our eyes in the morning with no thought of whether we will see. We take these blessings for granted … until they are not.

Someone in some place in the world is being challenged on all the above. They understand these things are not automatically granted, so when they receive more time, water, food, or sight they are grateful. The writer of Psalm 136 prompts us to acknowledge that the blessings of God are due to the enduring love of God. We, of course, can expect God to provide for us because He said He would, but we receive it from a place of humility and not entitlement, understanding that it flows from His mercy. The King James Version says, "oh give thanks unto the Lord, for He is good; for His mercy endureth forever". We don't deserve mercy. We don't deserve to walk with God. So, we are thankful for the opportunity to be in relationship with Him.

Stay grateful. We pray that our walk with God brings us blessing, long life, unspeakable joy, and perfect peace. And it will, most of the time. But as you walk with Him today, be humbly aware that it is a privilege. When you count it as a privilege, you won't miss your time of prayer. When you count it as a privilege, you will give attention to your walk and take care of it. You will protect it, cherish it, and delight in it. Give Him extra thanks today for things you haven't thanked Him for in a long time. Take nothing for granted. Stay grateful.

152 LOVE HIM, CHOOSE HIM

"The devil led Him up to a high place and showed Him in an instant all the kingdoms of the world. And he said to Him, "I will give You all their authority and splendor; it has been given to me, and I can give it to anyone I want to. If You worship me, it will all be Yours." Jesus answered, "It is written: 'Worship the Lord your God and serve Him only.'"

– Luke 4:5-8 (NIV)

Our love relationship with God is definitely a two-way street. He first loved us and then chose us. We then get the opportunity to love Him and choose Him back. When Jesus said the disciples didn't choose Him, but He chose them, He was talking about initial calling. We can't come to Jesus unless we have been called to Him, but once that happens, we are still free will beings. God has given you the ability to choose and He doesn't take it for granted that you have chosen to love Him and serve Him.

Jesus was in perfect love relationship with the Father, and He gives us our example as to how we should respond to anything that tempts us to choose something other than Him. Satan offered Jesus an easy route to getting the kingdoms of the world, however Jesus chose His Father above even His own comfort. He chose His Father above His own life. He determined to hold to the command of God that we worship and serve the only True and Living God. Because He always did His Father's will, they remained in a love relationship. God was well pleased with Jesus because Jesus always chose Him first.

Today, take comfort in knowing that God acknowledges that you have chosen to love Him. He is excited that you want to walk with Him. He knows that you have choices every day. It wouldn't be true love if you didn't have a choice. He laid before all of us good and evil, blessing and curses, life and death. He tells us to choose. He wants us to choose life, blessing and good, but He won't force us to. When we choose Him over, and over again, He grants us favor and calls us friend. When you have a choice today between God's will and something or someone else, choose Him … today and every day.

Naida M. Parson, Ph.D

153 FOREKNOWN AND PREDESTINED

"For those God foreknew He also predestined to be conformed to the image of His Son, that He might be the firstborn among many brothers and sisters. And those He predestined, He also called; those He called, He also justified; those He justified, He also glorified."

– Romans 8:29-30 (NIV)

It is so good to be known! To have someone who knows you, understands you, can tell what you're thinking, and what you're going to say is one of the human joys of relationship. But to be foreknown is even more amazing! God not only knows us, but He has known us from before we were created. He planned us and chose us before the world began. Just as God is pleased that we chose Him over ourselves, and over what the world has to offer, we should never take it for granted that He has chosen us before there *was* us.

Paul writes to the Romans that God foreknew us and then predestined us to be like Jesus. Because He knew we would receive the gospel, He made sure He found us, called us, saved us, and made us right with God. In the end, we will be translated into His glorious eternal kingdom and live forever with the Lord. We were not able to do any of this for ourselves. It is a gift from God. It is grace. It is mercy. It is love.

In your prayer time today, be in awe of the fact that you are one of the few human beings chosen to live your life in a love relationship with God. You have been invited to walk with Him through no goodness of your own. There is nothing special about you over any other human being in the world, except that He foreknew you lovingly walking with Him, and He had to have you in His life, so to speak. Appreciate that to its fullness. Never, ever take it for granted. Never lose sight of the privilege of this Enoch experience.

154 FACING LIFE ... TOGETHER

"When you pass through the waters, I will be with you; and when you pass through the rivers, they will not sweep over you. When you walk through the fire, you will not be burned; the flames will not set you ablaze. For I am the Lord your God, the Holy One of Israel, your Savior; I give Egypt for your ransom, Cush and Seba in your stead. Since you are precious and honored in My sight, and because I love you, I will give people in exchange for you, nations in exchange for your life. Do not be afraid, for I am with you; I will bring your children from the east and gather you from the west."

— Isaiah 43:2-5 (NIV)

Sometimes when bad things happen to Christians, we get angry with God and feel that either He is the One causing the pain, or that He is on the sidelines watching it all from afar. Life circumstances are going to happen to everyone, and Christians are not exempt. The Bible never hid that from us, but for some reason, trouble often interrupts our walk with God. The attitude God would prefer us to have is that when things happen to us, think of them as happening to you and God together. Not that life happens to God, but that because it's happening to you, and you are walking closely with Him, it's like it has happened to you both.

God sees it that way. It's part of being in a relationship. He has chosen not to shield us from all the effects of being in a fallen world with a fallen nature, but He wanted Isaiah to tell His people that "when you pass through the waters, I will be with you; and when you pass through the rivers, they will not sweep over you. When you walk through the fire, you will not be burned; the flames will not set you ablaze. For I am the Lord your God, the Holy One of Israel, your Savior". Notice that He did not say He would stop the waters, or the rivers, or the fire. But He did promise to be with us in them, and that because He is present with us, the circumstances of life can only have minimal effects on us. They will not destroy us because God is in there with us.

Today, if you are going through any difficulty, don't see it as happening to only you as you reach out to God for help. See it as two friends walking together, so when trouble comes, He is already there. But the One you are walking with is the Almighty God. He will handle anything that comes your way. It can only have a limited effect. And know that whatever He does allow to happen is carefully calculated by Him in advance. He is never caught off guard. He always sees it coming and He sees it going…the waters, the rivers, and the fire.

Naida M. Parson, Ph.D

155 GOD IS NOT AGAINST YOU

"Though He slay me, yet will I hope in Him; I will surely defend my ways to His face. Indeed, this will turn out for my deliverance, for no godless person would dare come before Him!"

– Job 13:15-16 (NIV)

One of the most puzzling books in the Bible is the book of Job. It is rich in concepts of what it means to walk with God, but it also shares some harsh realities about the sovereignty of God and His option to test and try us. It challenges our view of a loving God Who will only do us good. It's important that we do not create God in our image. We are created in His and He is Who He is. Our minute minds can never phantom every nuance of what He decides to do or allow. There are a few stories in the Bible I would have left out to make God more marketable as I present Him to the world. The story of Job is one of them!

The basic progression of the story is that Satan asked to destroy Job's life, and God let him, in order to test Job's loyalty. At this point in the story, Job gives us a true picture of what it means to walk with God and be at odds with Him at the same time. What God allowed was as bad as it gets. Death would have been better and Job states that throughout the book in a few different ways. On the one hand, he says that even though he is convinced that this is God killing him, he will continue to trust Him. On the other hand, he says he will defend himself to God's face. He believes that an audience with God will end up well for him because he is a godly man. Job didn't understand how God could have turned on him like this, but he also knew that the God he was in relationship with could be trusted and was ultimately on his side.

When life takes a tragic turn, it's important that you don't pit God against you. When bad things happen, don't see that as God moving against you. You may not be able to figure Him out but know that He can be trusted and that He trusts you to stay loyal to Him. Trusting God's ability is easy. Trusting His love is a given. Trusting His character is a byproduct of knowing Him. But trusting His judgment is one of the most difficult levels of faith to achieve. Tragedy is going to come to you in this life in some form. You live in a fallen world. But when it comes, the greatest test of the authenticity of your walk with God is your ability to trust His judgment. Don't make it about you against Him. You are still in this together. Make the decision today that when something happens in this walk that you don't like or understand, even with tears in your eyes and maybe frustration in your heart, you will keep walking.

156 TESTED ... BUT, IN IT TOGETHER

"No temptation has overtaken you except what is common to mankind. And God is faithful; He will not let you be tempted beyond what you can bear. But when you are tempted, He will also provide a way out so that you can endure it."

– 1 Corinthians 10:13 (NIV)

You and God are in this together. Walking with Him means that He is concerned and involved in every area of your life. Even when you are being tested and tempted, He is right there providing a way out so that you can handle it. Not only does He provide the way out, but through His indwelling Spirit, He will lead you right to the escape hatch! There are things that are just common to life on planet earth. Some of those things are going to be hard. God wants you to trust Him when these things are allowed into your life. Always think of it as you and God going through them together.

In this scripture, Paul lets the Corinthians know that even though hard times happen, God is faithful. He can be depended on. He can be trusted. He has it all in control. He allows us to be tested so that we can be perfected. You won't know that you are truly loving unless, every now and then, He allows you to be hurt. You won't know that you need to work on your patience, unless He lets someone torment you. You won't know you are truly free from that addiction, unless He allows you to be confronted with it over, and over, again. However, you can trust that He will not allow any test to come that He has not made sure was able to be passed.

Today, be more aware of the times that you are tested and tempted and be sensitive to the leading of God as to how to handle it. Don't see it as God sitting back waiting to see if you're going to blow it, so He can accuse you of not loving Him enough. He is not testing you to watch you fail. He is allowing you to be tested to develop you. He is faithful to you. He is right there to help you pass the test. He wants you to succeed because He is on this walk with you and what happens to you happens to you both. So, listen and perceive more closely during the times you are tested. There is a way of escape and God is there pointing to it.

Naida M. Parson, Ph.D

157 THE DEVIL HAS NO POWER HERE

"See, it is I Who created the blacksmith who fans the coals into flame and forges a weapon fit for its work. And it is I Who have created the destroyer to wreak havoc; no weapon forged against you will prevail, and you will refute every tongue that accuses you. This is the heritage of the servants of the Lord, and this is their vindication from Me," declares the Lord."

— Isaiah 54:16-17 (NIV)

One of the best things about walking humbly with God is that there is nothing the devil can do about it. He has no power here. Our walk with God is personal and private. The devil can try to lure us away, seduce us away, or talk us into walking away, but he is hopelessly helpless on the sidelines, watching one love affair after another develop and thrive. Once God chooses you and you say yes, it's a done deal. The devil has no say so.

Isaiah quotes God in the 54th chapter of his book as saying, "no weapon forged against you will prevail". During the time this was written, God's people had strayed so much and were going down a wrong path. They were allowed to be conquered by outside nations, but after their punishment, He already was planning their comeback. God declared that since He made the guy who makes all the weapons, and He made the guy who uses all the weapons, He can guarantee that there is no weapon made that would be victorious against them. Once they are restored to their place in God, the enemy would have no power to destroy them.

Today, you can enjoy your walk with God with no fear that your enemy can stop you. The devil has no power here. No weapon can keep you from walking together. There are weapons formed and they will be used, but none will be able to prevail. Be confident in your relationship with God today. There is so much forgiveness and grace that you have no need to fear failing Him or being abandoned. And there is nothing your enemy can do about it.

158 THE ENOCH EXPERIENCE: ONE FINAL NOTE

"When Enoch had lived 65 years, he became the father of Methuselah. After he became the father of Methuselah, Enoch walked faithfully with God 300 years and had other sons and daughters. Altogether, Enoch lived a total of 365 years. Enoch walked faithfully with God; then he was no more because God took him away."

– Genesis 5:21-24 (NIV)

As we have learned in this devotional, there is not much the bible says about Enoch except that he walked with God. The writer of Hebrews says that "by faith Enoch was taken from this life, so that he did not experience death. He could not be found, because God had taken him away. For before he was taken, he was commended as one who pleased God." Other than one more reference of Him prophesying, that's about it. But, what a glorious testimony! He walked with God and pleased Him. That is all that God requires of us; to do what's right, to be good to people, and walk with Him.

All of us will have different paths to take. Some of us will do great things and be known worldwide. Some of us will do great things in our communities, or in our homes. There were great men of God throughout the bible, but only Enoch went on a walk with God and disappeared. Elijah had all the fame and greatness and left on a fiery chariot. Moses was said to have died, but his body was never found. He was also famous and great. And then there is Enoch. The experience He had is one we all can have. Walking with God and pleasing Him is what this devotional has been all about. You have, in these short essays, a journey to experience God in a richer and fuller way.

One final note. I believe God is saying to all of us, His chosen children, "I will take you places and show you things if you will walk with Me, just like I did Enoch." Who knows what Enoch saw, or where he went, but I'm excited to see what else my journey with God is going to show me, and what other wonderful places we will go! My favorite activity in the world is to go outside and literally walk with God. I would love to end my earthly life that way. Just be out walking and talking with God and suddenly find myself in a new dimension, but still on my walk! So, I'm excited for every soul that reads this. After this, you should have a deeper relationship and a more intimate walk with God. May your journey be eternal and full of joy.

Naida M. Parson, Ph.D

Printed in the United States
by Baker & Taylor Publisher Services